T0323609

Cambridge Elements

Elements in the Problems of God
edited by
Michael L. Peterson
Asbury Theological Seminary

GOD AND THE PROBLEM
OF EPISTEMIC DEFEATERS

Joshua C. Thurow
The University of Texas at San Antonio

CAMBRIDGE
UNIVERSITY PRESS

CAMBRIDGE
UNIVERSITY PRESS

Shaftesbury Road, Cambridge CB2 8EA, United Kingdom

One Liberty Plaza, 20th Floor, New York, NY 10006, USA

477 Williamstown Road, Port Melbourne, VIC 3207, Australia

314–321, 3rd Floor, Plot 3, Splendor Forum, Jasola District Centre,
New Delhi – 110025, India

103 Penang Road, #05–06/07, Visioncrest Commercial, Singapore 238467

Cambridge University Press is part of Cambridge University Press & Assessment,
a department of the University of Cambridge.

We share the University's mission to contribute to society through the pursuit of
education, learning and research at the highest international levels of excellence.

www.cambridge.org
Information on this title: www.cambridge.org/9781009539029

DOI: 10.1017/9781009270649

© Joshua C. Thurow 2024

First published 2024

A catalogue record for this publication is available from the British Library

ISBN 978-1-009-53902-9 Hardback
ISBN 978-1-009-27062-5 Paperback
ISSN 2754-8724 (online)
ISSN 2754-8716 (print)

God and the Problem of Epistemic Defeaters

Elements in the Problems of God

DOI: 10.1017/9781009270649
First published online: December 2024

Joshua C. Thurow
The University of Texas at San Antonio

Author for correspondence: Joshua C. Thurow, Joshua.thurow@utsa.edu

Abstract: Any modern, moderately intellectually mature (MMIM) believer in God faces a variety of epistemic defeaters of their belief in God. Epistemic defeaters challenge the rationality of a belief. After explaining the notion of a defeater and discussing various ways and targets of defeat, this Element categorizes the many defeaters of belief in God into four classes: rebutting, undercutting, base defeaters, and competence defeaters. Then, several general defeaters of theistic belief are examined in some detail: the superfluity argument, the problem of unpossessed evidence, various forms of debunking arguments, and a cumulative case competence defeater. The typical MMIM believer, it is argued, has resources to resist these defeaters, although the cumulative case competence defeater has some force. The strength of its force depends on the strength of grounds for theistic belief and of various defeaters and deflectors for the competence defeater. No easy general defeater of theistic belief is found.

This Element also has a video abstract: www.cambridge.org/
EPOG_Thurow_Abstarct

Keywords: defeaters, rationality, justification, problems for theism, rationality of faith

ISBNs: 9781009539029 (HB), 9781009270625 (PB), 9781009270649 (OC)
ISSNs: 2754-8724 (online), 2754-8716 (print)

Contents

1 What Is the Problem?

In short, the problem is this: Any modern, moderately intellectually mature believer in God faces a variety of challenges to the rationality/reasonableness[1] of their belief in God. These sorts of challenges are called "epistemic defeaters." These challenges may be strong enough to prevent them from being able to know various things they initially thought they knew about God (such as that God exists). Some of the challenges have been around for centuries, and others have arisen or become prominent more recently. Many of these challenges are threatening even if we assume that believers in God typically have strong justification for their belief.

A modern, moderately intellectually mature (MMIM, for short) believer in God is a believer who

(i)   moderately understands their belief in God (and related beliefs),
(ii) understands to some moderate degree how those beliefs fit together,
(iii) is moderately aware of the dominant scientific understanding of the world and the place of humans in it,
(iv) is moderately aware of the outlines of the range of diverse religious stances in the world, and
(v)   is moderately intellectually competent at forming and maintaining their beliefs (and thus possesses, moderately, intellectual virtues such as curiosity, carefulness, humility, and open-mindedness).[2]

The term "moderate" is intended to depict a degree of possession that is typical of an educated young adult who has the qualities described. A MMIM believer is an idealization, to be sure. Many believers are not MMIM – children, many adolescents, some particularly sheltered adults, and some people with mental disabilities. But I wager that most believers are MMIM (or approximately so), and most of those who aren't will one day become (or once were) MMIM. And many of the rest fail to be MMIM because they suffer from various intellectual vices.

Consider the plight of a MMIM believer in God.[3] As most people do, they of course think their beliefs are true, care about their beliefs – especially core beliefs such as religious and moral beliefs – being true, and think of themselves, and wish to be thought of, as rational in holding their beliefs (Wuthnow 2012).

---

[1] I will mostly use these terms interchangeably; exceptions will be noted.
[2] See King (2021) for a clear and accessible introduction to the intellectual virtues. King aims to describe what he calls "the excellent mind"; I'm aiming for a lot less – the moderately competent mind.
[3] By "God" we will mean "the omnipotent, omniscient, all good creator of the universe and its inhabitants." Jews, Christians, and Muslims all believe in God, in this sense. Anselm's perfect being – a being than which none greater can be conceived – is also God in this sense.

However, it is hard to be a MMIM believer. In particular, MMIM believers face various challenges to the rationality of their belief in God (and related beliefs).

Take Kristi, a typical MMIM Christian believer in God.[4] Kristi believes that God is all knowing and in some sense in control of every facet of the universe, but Kristi also believes that she is responsible for her actions and has sinned against God. Kristi notices a tension here (a classic tension that has long been discussed in philosophical/theological literature, although Kristi probably knows little to nothing of this literature): How can she be responsible for her actions if God knows exactly what she is going to do ahead of time? Does God's foreknowledge conflict with her freedom, and thus her responsibility for her actions? Kristi also notices that the world is full of evil and some of it is hard to reconcile with her beliefs about God: Her uncle, a devout Christian and good man, died in a car wreck leaving behind a family; natural disasters kill many people and destroy the homes and livelihood of others; and diseases strike communities with no apparent regard for their moral qualities. Kristi here wrestles with the problem of evil. Kristi notices that the Bible seems full of miraculous events and God or angels speaking to people, and yet she doesn't see much of that today. When she does hear of such claims she tends to be somewhat skeptical. But if she's skeptical of such claims today, why should she so readily accept miraculous claims from ancient texts? Kristi here wrestles with the problem of whether it is rational to believe in miracles. She sees that some of the distinctive moral claims made by her brand of Christianity are deeply contested by others in her society and she herself feels that some of her society's objections to these claims have force. These are all potential problems for Christianity that arise from the specific claims made by Christianity.

There are other more general problems that Kristi is aware of. She knows that other people reject Christianity, and many people accept other religions. And she knows that many of these people seem reasonable, devout, and good. What reason does she have to think she is correct in believing in Christianity whereas all these other people are incorrect? She is aware of the fact that science is very successful at explaining events in the world – even events that for much of human history seemed mysterious. She wonders: Can science explain every

---

[4] I take it that belief that God exists is distinct from, though necessary for belief in God. Belief in God involves positive affection for God and trust in God. Both attitudes presume believing that God exists, but go well beyond merely believing that God exists (Price 1965). Belief in God is perhaps typically grounded in (putative) acquaintance with God (see Moser 2010 for discussion of acquaintance with God). Belief in God is threatened by defeaters because belief in God presumes belief that God exists. If defeaters succeed in knocking out belief that, belief in is knocked out as well. Even if belief that isn't knocked out, a believer in God will experience a defeater as a challenge because they will see it as a potential threat to their belief in God; they'll see it as something that, if undefeated, indicates they shouldn't believe that God exists and thus shouldn't believe in God.

event in the world? If so, maybe God isn't as active in the world as she thought. She's even vaguely aware that some scientists have given evolutionary explanations for why humans hold religious beliefs – including belief in God! Could it be, she wonders, that her beliefs about God don't reflect reality at all, but that she holds those beliefs for reasons entirely unrelated to the truth of the matter?

Charles Taylor argues that most people in the West live in a secular age – a society where belief in God "is understood to be one option among others, and frequently not the easiest to embrace" (Taylor, 2007: 3). The things mentioned above are part of what makes theism difficult to embrace, but Taylor diagnoses the difficulty in a view modern westerners have about the self. They view their self as "buffered." A buffered self privileges itself over the world outside the self by treating things as meaningful, valuable, or as ends worth pursuing only insofar as the self bestows meaning/value/worth (Taylor, 2007: 38). A buffered self views itself as choosing to be open to other things and their value. This is to be contrasted with what Taylor calls a "porous self" which views itself as innately, without any control, vulnerable to the influence of foreign forces that can both move the self and bestow or bring meaning/value/worth. Christianity – and other theistic views – fits better with seeing the self as porous as God himself is viewed as the source of all goodness, value, and ultimate meaning and God knows everything about all human selves and can influence them directly. Assuming that Taylor's views are correct, Kristi likely views herself as buffered, and so finds it difficult to accept the Christian God, which appears to threaten her view of herself. This isn't just a psychological obstacle for Kristi, but also an epistemological obstacle if she has good reason to think that selves are buffered. She surely has good testimonial reasons for thinking this as most folks in her community (even modern Western religious folks, Taylor argues), have such a view.

This is but a brief survey of some of the challenges Kristi faces in embracing Christianity.[5] Some amount to psychological or social pressures pushing against Christianity, or certain aspects of Christianity, or pushing toward other views. But others are epistemic – that is, they are challenges that indicate there is something bad about Kristi's religious beliefs when evaluated from the perspective of attempting to accurately apprehend the way the world is: either her religious beliefs are false, or she lacks good reason to think they are accurate (or she has less reason than she used to have, or thought she had), or she does not know them to be true.

The notion of a defeater is useful for categorizing and understanding the force of these different epistemic challenges to religious belief. After describing defeaters in the next section, we will then categorize a variety of defeaters for

---

[5] Clearly some of the same, or similar, problems face other theistic religions such as Judaism and Islam.

belief in God. We will then evaluate in greater detail just a few of these defeaters – in particular, some defeaters that pose a challenge to a wide range of beliefs about God from many different religious traditions.

2 Defeaters

The notion of a defeater originates in the work of twentieth-century epistemologist John Pollock on defeasible reasoning. He defines it as follows:

> If M is a reason for S to believe Q, a state M* is a *defeater* for this reason if and only if the combined state consisting of being in both the state M and the state M* at the same time is not a reason for S to believe Q (Pollock & Cruz, 1999: 195).[6]

Pollock's notion of defeaters is defined in a background view that centralizes reasons as the determinants of justification.[7] In this view, one's beliefs are justified provided they are supported by adequate reasons. Defeaters are states that, combined with one's original reasons for believing Q, prevent those reasons from remaining as reasons. Pollock describes two sorts of defeaters. The first, a *rebutting defeater*, is a reason for believing not-Q. If M* is a rebutting defeater with sufficient strength, then M – a reason for believing Q – and M* will together not be a reason for believing Q as M* will balance against M. The second, an *undercutting defeater*, doesn't directly provide any evidence against Q; rather, undercutting defeaters are reasons to doubt or deny that one would not be in M unless Q were true. Others describe them a little differently: either M* indicates that M does not adequately support Q in the circumstances, or M* indicates that M does not make Q likely to be true in the circumstances.

In this view, reasons are sort of like forces that push around where one's belief should be.[8] A strong reason for believing p is like a fan blowing a small plastic toy across a track and the movement of the plastic toy in a certain direction is like belief in p being justified (how justified is sort of like how forcefully the toy is moved). A defeater, then, is something that prevents the motion of the toy. A rebutting defeater would be like having another fan on the other end of the track, blowing directly with equal force against the first fan. Now the toy doesn't move at all, and so belief in p isn't justified. However, note: The first fan is still on. It is still providing a force in a certain direction; it's just that the force vector is countered by an equal and opposite vector. Likewise, rebutting defeaters

---

[6] Sudduth (2022) and Piazza (2021) provide useful overviews of the literature on epistemic defeaters.

[7] Beddor (2021) calls this the Reasons First tradition, no doubt to contrast it with the Knowledge First approach to epistemology spearheaded by Timothy Williamson (2015).

[8] Reasons do not necessarily push one's belief to where it should be. Other factors – biases and inattention, for example – may prevent one's belief from being where the reasons indicate it should.

leave the strength of the initial reason intact. They just counter it with equal and opposite reasons. (Of course, there can be partial defeaters, which are opposite in direction but of lesser force.) An undercutting defeater would be like turning off the first fan, or rotating it so that it isn't pointing down the track. Here, no additional force is applied to the toy; rather the force of the initial fan is modified (removed or redirected).

The distinction between rebutting and undercutting defeaters is fairly intuitive from simple examples. Suppose I'm wondering where I placed my keys. I seem to remember putting them in the drawer of the stand by the front door – which I know, from memory, is where I usually place them. These memories are reasons to believe my keys are in the drawer. Now let's imagine two different cases. In the first case, I go look in the drawer and I do not see the keys there. This perceptual experience is a reason to think my keys are not in the drawer, thus it is a rebutting defeater of my memory-based reason for thinking my keys are in the drawer. In the second case, I realize that when I last came in the house I had a bunch of stuff in my hands and I was in a hurry and tired and I know that, in those circumstances, I am prone to putting my keys down absentmindedly in various other places but – because I usually place my keys in the drawer – my mind later falsely appears to remember placing them in the drawer. All this evidence about the special circumstances in this scenario provides reason for thinking that my apparent memory isn't a good indicator that the keys are in the drawer. This evidence thus is an undercutting defeater of my memory-based reason for thinking the keys are in the drawer. Notice that in this latter case, my knowledge about the special circumstances is not evidence that my keys are not in the drawer. Maybe they are, maybe they aren't; maybe I actually do have a memory of putting them there; maybe given the circumstances my memory is faulty. I can't tell which it is and I don't know how likely it is that the keys are in the drawer.[9]

Defeaters can themselves be defeated. Suppose, to modify the latter example above, my spouse tells me, "Yes, you were in a hurry and tired, but nevertheless you were clearly really on top of things. Those factors didn't seem to be affecting you at the time." My spouse – who knows me well – provides testimony that rebuts my reason for thinking my memory may have been faulty in the circumstances. This restores my apparent memory as a reason for thinking my keys are in the drawer.

Defeater defeaters could be defeated by a further defeater, which could also be defeated, and so on. A reason for a belief held by a certain person is *ultimately undefeated* provided it retains its justificational force (or perhaps

---

[9] I could keep a track record of how often, in these circumstances, I fail to place my keys in the drawer. If the track record indicated that I usually fail to place my keys in the drawer in these circumstances (and I was aware of this track record), then I would have a rebutting defeater as well as an undercutting defeater.

a reduced, but still positive justificational force) after considering all other relevant evidence/reasons possessed by the person.[10] A person's belief will be *propositionally justified* if and only if it is supported by sufficiently strong ultimately undefeated reason(s) possessed by the person. Propositional justification concerns whether a proposition is supported by adequate reasons for a person. It is distinct from doxastic justification, which concerns whether a person's belief is based on adequate reasons. A person's belief is *doxastically justified* if and only if the person's belief is based on sufficiently strong ultimately undefeated reasons.

Shortly we'll discuss a few other possible kinds of defeat, but first we should address a couple of objections facing Pollock's account of defeat. First, Chandler (2013) provides a counterexample wherein a defeater D defeats the force of a reason R for believing p, while providing its own support for p. The combination of D&R constitutes a reason to believe p, and yet D seems to defeat R, contrary to Pollock's definition of defeating a reason. This appears not to present a devastating problem for Pollock's general approach to defeaters since an alternate definition seems acceptable:

> If M is a reason for S to believe Q, a state M* is a *defeater* for this reason if and only if in the combined state consisting of being in both the state M and the state M* at the same time, M is not a reason that would justify belief Q.[11]

In Chandler's case, R is not a reason that would justify belief Q, although there is another reason to believe Q: D itself. This definition also allows that undercutting and rebutting defeaters are two different ways of M not being a reason that would justify Q in light of a defeater: because M has no justificational force in M&M*, or because M's justificational force is rebutted by M*'s force (respectively).

The second objection is more concerning. Pollock's approach to defeaters takes reasons to be what grounds justified beliefs. This approach is conducive to evidentialist, internalist approaches to epistemology such as Conee and Feldman's (2004). However, many contemporary epistemologists are externalists, and non-evidentialist. In their view, reasons do not play an essential role in justifying a belief; rather, a belief is justified when it is the result of a process that is suitably truth-conducive (e.g. reliable, safe, sensitive, or competent). These externalist epistemologies must provide an alternative account of defeat. Goldman's (1979) reliabilist account of defeat is particularly notable, although it also has faced

---

[10] Pollock (1987) defines ultimate defeat in terms of the technical notion of an inference branch being "in at a level." See Beddor (2021) for a helpful summary.

[11] Chandler offers a slightly different modified definition that may be equivalent to this definition, depending on how the notion of "a reason" is to be understood. Graham & Lyons (2021) provided a different Pollockian approach to defeat that also evades Chandler's counterexample.

objection (see Beddor 2015). Nevertheless, the worry for Pollock's definition is that it weds the notion of defeat too closely to a general epistemological approach that is highly contested, even though the notion of defeat should have a place in any epistemological theory.

Although Pollock's account of defeaters fits well with internalist evidentialist theories in epistemology, his account can also be built to fit with externalist non-evidentialist theories. Beddor (2021) defends what he calls "reasons reliabilism" according to which reasons for belief are identified with the inputs to reliable or conditionally reliable available belief-forming processes. Reasons reliabilism can simply import all of what Pollock says about defeaters, while giving a reliabilist account of reasons. Graham and Lyons (2021) propose instead to define defeaters in terms of warrants (rather than reasons), where to have a warrant to believe p is just to have prima facie propositional justification to believe p. Reasons can provide warrant, but there can be warrant without reasons, as with (in their view) non-inferential perceptual beliefs. Then they provide an externalist account of propositional justification. Their account of defeaters maintains the important structural features of Pollock's account, simply replacing the notion of reasons with the notion of warrants. These theories may face their own objections, but their existence and promise indicate that Pollock's general approach to defeaters isn't clearly hostile or unfavorable to externalist, non-evidentialist epistemologies. Furthermore, we can flip this objection on its head. Pollock's general approach intuitively accounts well for the phenomena of defeat, and thus a good epistemological theory should be able to accommodate it (or one much like it).

As we've seen, Pollock defines the notion of a reason being defeated; however we can also talk about our justification, our belief, and even our knowledge being defeated. We will also want to distinguish between the defeated state (e.g. a reason, justification, belief, and knowledge) and the mode of defeat – that is, the way the state is defeated. Pollock focuses on one defeated state – reasons – and mentions two modes of defeat: rebutting and undercutting. Definitions of other defeated states will reveal additional modes of defeat.

Here are some Pollock-inspired definitions of defeat of propositional and doxastic justification:

> If S is propositionally justified in believing p in virtue of state J, where J includes the total relevant reasons possessed by S aside from D, then state D is a defeater of this state of being propositionally justified if and only if the combined state consisting of being in both the state J and the state D at the same time does not propositionally justify p.
>
> If S is doxastically justified in believing p based on state J, where J includes the total relevant reasons possessed by S aside from D, then state D is

> a defeater of this state of being doxastically justified if and only if in the combined state consisting of being in both the state J and the state D at the same time, S is not doxastically justified in believing p.[12]

These notions are broader than reasons defeat because one of one's reasons could be defeated while others remain undefeated and thus one could remain propositionally and doxastically justified while having a reasons defeater. Thus the state of being justified will be defeated only if one's total reasons are taken into consideration (this is why J is defined the way it is). We could also define notions of propositional justification or doxastic justification being defeated. These notions allow that you can have justification without being justified, and that a source of justification can be defeated while you remain justified. It should be fairly clear how to define these notions given the definitions of reasons defeat and defeat of being justified.

Rebutting and undercutting defeaters are also modes for defeating the states of being propositionally or doxastically justified. But there is another mode of defeat for doxastic justification: defeat that changes the basis for one's belief. One could cease to be doxastically justified based on J if one ceased to base one's belief on J. The state that caused this to occur would count as a defeater according to this definition; we can call it a *"base defeater."* The nature of the basing relation is disputed (see Korcz 2021), but it is fairly easy to see how base defeat could occur. A person could hold a belief on the basis of good reasons, but then later encounter poor reasons for the same belief that are, for some reason, much more attractive to the person and so their basis for the belief shifts to the new, poor reasons. Imagine a person who already has a good reason for thinking a certain politician is corrupt, but who is convinced by poor reasons persuasively presented for believing that the politician is corrupt because of their participation in some elaborate conspiracy. As a result, the person fixates on the conspiracy theory, which guides her belief while the previous good reasons cease having any continuing effect. She may remain propositionally justified in believing that the politician is corrupt (her overall reasons still support this claim), but she is no longer doxastically justified.

Knowledge can also be defeated. One could acquire strong evidence against a proposition that one formerly knew. One could acquire an undercutting defeater: Some information that, together with one's former grounds for belief, now no longer supports that belief in a way that amounts to knowledge. Different theories of knowledge will offer different accounts of when and how this occurs. And one could acquire a base defeater where one's new base does not ground knowledge.

---

[12] As with Pollock's definitions, these define full defeat; partial defeat is possible as well.

Note that the term "defeater" is used in certain theories of knowledge to describe something quite distinct from how we are using the term here. In the "No Defeaters" theory of knowledge, one knows p (roughly) provided there is no fact such that – if one were aware of it – one would cease to be justified in believing p. A defeater, in this sense, prevents knowledge from being had, rather than eliminating a prior state of knowledge. Defeaters, in this sense, also can be completely outside of the subject's mind whereas defeaters, as we are characterizing them, are mental states (although we'll shortly examine a kind of defeater that isn't a mental state but is something one should be aware of).

We can also speak of a belief being defeated. Sometimes we might say "your belief is defeated" as shorthand for "your doxastic justification is defeated" or "your knowledge is defeated," expecting then that the person will go ahead and give up their belief (or reduce confidence if it is a partial defeater). But there are situations where a person has a belief that is not justified or known, and yet we can say "your belief is defeated." Plainly in these situations, we mean something different than "your doxastic justification/knowledge is defeated." We may neither know nor care whether their belief was initially justified/known; we may think that the person nevertheless has a defeater and as a result they should give up their belief. Here the defeater doesn't take away an initial positive epistemic status (i.e. being doxastically justified or having knowledge); rather, the defeater indicates that the person lacked justification/knowledge.

> If S's belief B lacks positive epistemic status but S bases B on grounds G that S takes to justify B (or to ground knowledge), then state D defeats B if and only if D provides strong reason to think that G does not ground positive epistemic status for B.

I'll call this mode of defeat, *status-revealing defeat*. Status-revealing defeat comes in many flavors. Something like rebutting, undercutting, and base defeaters can all provide status-revealing defeat. You might possess a reason that would rebut or undercut your grounds if your grounds were on their own to provide the justification/knowledge you thought they provided. Here no actual reasons or positive epistemic states are defeated – because you didn't have any to start with – but hypothetical reasons and positive epistemic states are defeated: the ones you have considered to be good grounds, hypothetically taken to be as good as you think they are. Alternatively, you might possess a reason for thinking that your actual grounds are some part of G and that part doesn't amount to good grounds for B.

Another variety of status-revealing defeat resembles undercutting defeat: having a reason to think that G is not good grounds for positive epistemic status. If G in fact was not good grounds, then no positive epistemic status was undermined (nor was a reason undermined). However, once you acquire this defeater, G is revealed to not be good grounds and should you rationally respond to the defeater, you no longer will rely on G. This defeater (and the undercutting-like defeater mentioned in the previous paragraph) and undercutting defeaters all show that the agent should not base her belief on some grounds by showing that those grounds do not suffice for justification/knowledge. The difference is that, with an under-cutting defeater, the grounds were good grounds (the defeater set aside), whereas with this defeater, the grounds were not good grounds (even setting the defeater aside).

There is another mode of defeat that has been at the center of some controversy in epistemology: what Nathan Ballantyne (2019: 104ff) calls a *competence defeater.* Competence defeaters do not address your first-order evidence/reasons/grounds about the proposition in question; rather they address your competence in evaluat-ing your evidence/reasons/grounds. Plainly competence defeaters can at least sometimes result in doxastic justification defeat. Consider a case wherein a person has misevaluated their evidence: they think their evidence supports p when in fact it does not. However, the person has followed what they are justified in taking to be the canons of evidence evaluation to the best of their ability and they have reason for thinking they are generally reliable at evaluating where the evidence points when they follow these canons. This person has good reason to think they have evaluated the evidence properly; as a result they are doxastically justified in believing p, even though their first-order evidence about p does not support p. Their second-order evidence about their competence, together with their considered judgment about what the first-order evidence supports, supports p. In this case, should the person acquire a reason, D, to think that in fact, in this situation, they have not evaluated the evidence competently, their second-order evidence would be defeated, and thus their doxastic justification would also be defeated. D would thus function as a competence defeater.[13]

Arguably, reflective subjects – including those who are moderately intellec-tually mature – will have developed a sense of their competence on various issues and situations and their assessment of their competence is part of the grounds for their beliefs. If this is correct, reflective subjects will always need to be mindful of potential competence defeaters, as those defeaters can potentially knock out some of their grounds for their beliefs (even if their beliefs are true and have positive support).

---

[13] As a side note, cases like these show why it is wrong to characterize higher-order defeaters or competence defeaters as evidence one was never rational to begin with (contra Christensen 2010 and Lasonen-Aarnio 2012). In these cases, one has a competence defeater even though one was rational to begin with as one previously had evidence of one's competence and rightly relied on that evidentially supported competence in coming to believe p.

However, many epistemologists think that competence defeaters do more than this. They don't just knock out a person's belief in their competence with respect to p, but they rationally should knock out belief in p as well. Suppose I have an undefeated competence defeater with respect to p: that is, I have good reason for thinking that I am not competent at evaluating p in my current circumstances, and no defeater for this good reason. I then have no reason to think that my belief that p has been arrived at competently. I should thus think that my belief is not justified/rational/known. But then I shouldn't believe p. How could I, rationally, keep on believing p if my evidence indicates that I am not justified or rational in believing p?[14]

If this reasoning is correct, then even in cases where a person in fact has good overall reason for believing p and has competently evaluated the reasons, if that person were to acquire good reason for thinking he was not competent (of course, this reason would be misleading), then the person's belief that p would not be justified/rational/known – despite in fact having good reasons, competently evaluated.[15] Let's call these "misleading competence defeater cases."

Here is where controversy arises. Some philosophers reject the above description of people in misleading competence defeater cases. They say that people who have good overall reasons to believe p and have competently evaluated their reasons know (and may be justified in believing) p, despite having good reason for thinking they are not competent at evaluating p. They embrace what has become known as "level-splitting": you can know/be justified in believing p while being justified in believing that you are not justified in believing p. This view has been supported a couple of different ways. Lasonen-Aarnio (2012) argues that there is no plausible, coherent way to have a rule-based epistemology that embraces (1) a belief is rational only if it is the result of following the correct rules, and (2) a belief is rational only if one lacks evidence that it is rationally flawed. Lasonen-Aarnio (2010) argues that some plausible externalist theories (e.g. safety theories) of knowledge cannot account for various putative cases of defeat (including misleading competence defeater cases), and that this should not be seen as problematic. Baker-Hytch and Benton (2015) argue that all plausible theories of justification/knowledge either have internal problems or cannot account for various putative cases of defeat – including misleading competence defeater cases – and thus we should think that some of those putative cases of defeat are not genuine cases.

---

[14] This argument from the irrationality of epistemic akrasia (i.e. it is irrational to believe p while at the same time believing that your believing p is irrational) is given by many philosophers. For further discussion see, most notably, Horowitz (2014) and Christensen (2022).

[15] There are various accounts of why defeat occurs in misleading competence defeater cases. See Whiting (2020) for a summary.

Despite the arguments of their defenders, level-splitting views are not widely accepted, in part because they reject what seem to many to be very clear cases of defeat and because of the apparent inconsistency of at the same time believing p and believing that one's belief that p is irrational. However, for our purposes we needn't resolve this dispute, for defenders of level-splitting grant that there is something epistemically bad about continuing to believe p when one has good evidence that one is not competent in evaluating p. Lasonen-Aarnio (2010, 2021), for example, says that in these cases one believes unreasonably: that is, roughly, one believes in a way that is not knowledge conducive. And believing in this way is often criticizable. So even if we grant that knowledge and justification are not defeated in misleading competence defeater cases, people in those cases do not believe reasonably. They lack an epistemically valuable state that we ideally would like to have and typically think that we possess. And realizing that you lack that state will typically indicate that you should change your belief and how you act when your actions rely on that belief. This counts as a form of defeat for our purposes here.

The final mode of defeat that we shall discuss expands on what counts as defeating evidence. All the modes so far have presumed that, in order to defeat a person's belief/reason/justification/knowledge, a piece of evidence needs to be possessed by that person – that is, they need to be aware of the defeating evidence.[16] Several philosophers have argued that evidence one does not possess may also serve as a defeater. For instance, suppose that Jane has evidence that her daughter gets off school early today (her calendar says it is an early release day and she remembers putting the early release days in her calendar). So, Jane believes her daughter has an early release day today. However, the school changed the day to a full day to make up for a past cancelation, and they sent a robocall to parents' phones informing them of the change. Jane has ignored her phone and the messages she has received on it, so she is unaware of this information. Many people judge that in this case, Jane is not justified in believing that her daughter has an early release day today.[17] As Goldberg (2018, 2021) explains, Jane should have had the evidence from the robocall, and evidence that you should have had can defeat just as well as evidence you do have. Following Goldberg, we'll call these *normative defeaters*.[18]

---

[16] They don't need to be aware of it *as* defeating; evidence may defeat even if you are not aware that it defeats. But, you must (for the modes of defeat discussed so far) at least possess the evidence in order for it to potentially defeat. To be aware of evidence, one need not form a belief that one has the evidence. One can be aware of something, in the relevant sense, without forming a belief about it.

[17] See, e.g. Kornblith (1983), Meeker (2004), and Gibbons (2006) for similar examples.

[18] This is different from Lackey's (1999) notion of normative defeat, which has more to do with failing to acknowledge the significance of the defeating evidence you do possess. Lackey (and Bergmann 2005) endorses another mode of defeat that she calls doxastic defeat, which is supposed to be defeat for belief that p that arises due to another doubt or belief that indicates

It is somewhat controversial whether there are normative defeaters – that is, whether the evidence you should have possessed defeats your belief, reason, justification, or knowledge. But it is a common enough view that we shall take it seriously here as a potential defeater. Furthermore, even if normative defeaters don't defeat belief, reasons, justification, or knowledge, they seem epistemically significant. For we typically view our justified/known beliefs as non-fluky: that is, our being justified/having knowledge doesn't depend on being sheltered, disabled, ill-informed, or missing out on information we should know. If we have a normative defeater for a belief that p, then this ideal epistemic view of ourselves regarding believing p is inaccurate. Normative defeaters are thus threatening to our epistemic pictures of ourselves.

3 Map of Defeaters for Belief in God

In Section 1, I argued that a MMIM (modern, moderately intellectually mature) believer in God will wrestle with various defeaters for their belief in God. Section 2 has clarified the notion of a defeater, distinguishing various epistemic states that can be defeated and distinguishing various modes of defeat. Now we will map out a variety of defeaters for belief in God, categorizing them as we go by the modes of defeat they present.

Before presenting the map of defeaters, a few general comments are in order. First, some of the defeaters on the map will plainly be reason defeaters – that is, they purport to defeat a reason in favor of God's existence. Reason defeaters, as mentioned in Section 2, do not necessarily produce belief, justification, or knowledge defeaters, as a person might have other excellent grounds for their belief even if one of their reasons is in fact defeated. Whether reason defeat produces the other sorts of defeat depends on whether there are any undefeated reasons/grounds for thinking that God exists that remain after considering all the purported reason defeaters.

Second, many of the defeaters on the map will purport to be belief, justification, or knowledge defeaters. Which of those sorts of defeaters a believer has will depend upon the prior epistemic state of the believer. If the believer is a mere believer – that is, they are unjustified and lack knowledge – then the only state that could be defeated is their belief. If the believer knows that God exists and is justified in believing that God exists, then both their knowledge and justification may potentially be defeated. On most views of knowledge, justification defeat will also entail knowledge defeat, but the reverse is not true. That is, one's knowledge could be defeated while leaving one's justification intact.

---

that one's belief that p is false or unreliably formed. Graham & Lyons (2021) present deep objections to these modes of defeat.

This could happen if enough of one's reasons are defeated to drop the level of propositional justification below the knowledge threshold, but high enough to remain justified.

Third, whether a purported defeater actually defeats a person's belief in God will depend upon the believer's background mental profile – that is, their various mental states aside from the defeaters. This is so for at least two reasons. First, as mentioned above, which epistemic state is defeated depends on the prior epistemic state of the believer – whether, before considering the defeater, they knew or had a justified belief that God exists. Whether they knew or had a justified belief that God exists depends on their mental profile – their various reasons and experiences that may serve to ground their knowledge or justification. Second, as mentioned in Section 2, defeaters can themselves be defeated. And whether a believer has a defeater for the defeaters also depends on their various reasons and experiences.

Therefore, fourth, I will not be able to say here whether any of the purported defeaters on the map will in fact defeat any particular religious believer's epistemic state. That is because to do so I would have to know each aspect of the mental profile of that believer that can ground their belief in God or serve as a defeater–defeater. Most of us do not know other people's mental lives that intimately. Probably many of us do not have that intimate a knowledge of our own mental lives! In addition, I would have to know whether the believer initially justifiably believed or knew that God exists, and to do that I'd have to evaluate the various positive grounds for belief in God. I am not able to do that here either. The best I can do is this: describe, in a fairly general way, the relevant mental states of a typical MMIM believer and discuss whether and how the purported defeaters might defeat this typical believer's belief assuming, for the sake of argument, that their initial grounds sufficed for having a justified belief/knowledge that God exists. If, instead, we assume that their initial grounds do not render their belief justified or known, then the putative defeaters will instead at best be status-revealing.

Fifth, there are many religious beliefs regarding God that face putative defeaters, but here we are going to focus on defeaters for the claim that God exists. For those interested in evaluating other religious claims, the discussion here will provide a model that may prove useful for analyzing and evaluating defeaters for the religious claims that interest them.

Lastly, before presenting the map of defeaters, I want to describe, very broadly, a typical MMIM believer's grounds for believing that God exists. Work from the sociology and psychology of religion informs the picture I will paint.[19] However, for our purposes here it isn't necessary to have an empirically accurate picture of

---

[19] See Shermer (2003), Shtulman (2012), and Wuthnow (2012).

the typical MMIM believer. All we need is a picture that is roughly in the ballpark so that we can describe the defeaters faced by someone who comes close to matching this picture. We can then go on to discuss whether a person who matches the picture already has the resources to respond to the putative defeater, or whether there are any resources they might be able to acquire to address the defeater. It is less important, for our purposes, to accurately describe what resources the typical MMIM actually has.

A typical MMIM believer in God will have a variety of grounds for their belief.[20] These grounds fall into three broad classes: explanatory, experiential, and testimonial. Explanatory grounds indicate that God's existence and activity help explain various facts about the world. Cosmological arguments, design arguments, moral arguments and the like all fall under this class of grounds. Typically MMIM believers are not philosophically sophisticated. They are not aware of the various forms these arguments take or the history of discussion of them. However, typical MMIM believers are aware of the grounds that these arguments aim to articulate. Evans (2010) argues that these arguments are based on what he calls natural signs of God's existence: the existence, ordered structure, and moral character of the world. The philosophical arguments aim to articulate how these signs indicate that God exists, but you don't have to be aware of the arguments to recognize and follow the signs. Evans's view fits well with the fact that typical MMIM believers recognize these signs as reasons even though they often cannot (or cannot easily) articulate compelling arguments based on the signs. However, if these signs genuinely are signs of God's existence, Evans argues that it is rational to believe on the basis of an intuitive recognition of the signs, regardless of whether one can articulate an argument based on the signs.

Some historical arguments for miracles also count as explanatory reasons as they argue that certain historical events are best explained by the miraculous intervention of God. The most famous such arguments are Christian arguments for the resurrection of Jesus (Craig 1989; McGrew & McGrew 2009; Swinburne 2003). The historical evidence, such as it is, for miracles is of course not a natural sign of God's existence. Such evidence may amount to a sign, but only for those who are aware of the evidence and various background evidence needed to appreciate it. As any cursory scan of the literature on arguments for

---

[20] Reasons are often understood to inferentially justify beliefs, whereas grounds non-inferentially justify. I agree with the distinction, but nothing in my argument here depends on accurately classifying the religious grounds and reasons as grounds or reasons. And both can be subject to defeat. So I'll typically use the word "grounds" to mean grounds or reasons and I'll sometimes switch between both terms; nothing rides on my using one term over the other, unless context makes it clear I'm specifically discussing one of them.

the resurrection will show, they rely on information that it is doubtful many MMIM believers possess. However, MMIM believers are often aware of some of this evidence, as it is often partially encapsulated in religiously framed retellings of particularly significant putative miracles.

Experiential grounds include a wide range of experiences: of apparent miracles, of God's will or love or some other trait in a rich mystical experience, and of peace, comfort, love, guidance, and forgiveness that often come while praying. Mystical experiences are often difficult for the experiencer to describe and are fairly uncommon,[21] while experiences of peace, comfort, guidance, etc. while praying are common. Indeed, it is quite common for MMIM believers to seek out such experiences while praying and there is a long history of discussion about how to discern God's guiding will in these experiences (Alston 1991; Luhrmann 2012, 2020; Willard 2012).

Testimonial reasons are testimonial sources that in some way ground or purport to support belief in God. These can include the testimony of trusted people who report having had various religious experiences, the testimony of trusted people who have spent many years thinking through and practicing a religion, or the testimony of a religious text such as the Bible. Provided one has reason to trust these sources – and on most views of testimony it is fairly easy for us to acquire reason to trust testimony – one has testimonial grounds for one's belief.

I suggest that a MMIM believer will typically have some combination of the above three grounds. I do not assume that any of these grounds are more basic, psychologically or epistemologically. Psychologically, it is plausible that most MMIM believers begin with primarily testimonial grounds and later acquire experiential and explanatory grounds as they learn more about their religion and gain experience practicing it. Once a believer becomes MMIM, it seems plausible that their belief will come to rest on some combination of these three sorts of grounds. Their belief may later rest simply on their sense that, as far as they can tell, God's existence and providential action best "[make] sense of human life" (Donagan, 1999: 13), where all the above – and no doubt other – grounds are aspects of human life that God's existence explains well. Surely most MMIM believers do not explicitly, consciously, run an inference to the best explanation style argument for God's existence from the above features of human life. But we do have an intuitive sense of how well a set of beliefs hangs together and whether a given belief fits with other things we believe. This intuitive sense plausibly involves a sensitivity to how well God's existence explains, or makes sense of, these features of human life.

---

[21] Although not as uncommon as one might think. See, e.g. Hardy (1979), James (2002/1902), and Wiebe (1997).

This description of the grounds a typical MMIM believer has for believing that God exists is intended to be neutral about epistemological disputes regarding how a person is justified in believing, or knows, that something is the case. I make no assumptions about whether these grounds should be understood in an internalist or externalist way. Evidentialist internalists like Feldman and Swinburne will understand the grounds as evidence that may or may not support the proposition that God exists. Externalists like Goldman, Plantinga, and Sosa will understand the grounds as playing some key role in a process that may or may not be reliable, properly functioning, or apt in producing a true belief.[22] Internalist and externalist epistemologies both allow for the possibility of justification and knowledge defeaters, although they tend to give different analyses of how defeaters defeat.

Likewise, this description stays neutral regarding Reformed epistemology – the view that belief in God is (or can be) properly basic.[23] A belief is properly basic when it is epistemically proper (justified, rational, or known) and it is not based on an inference drawn from some other belief. In the description I gave of the typical MMIM believer, their grounds for belief in God may or may not be properly basic. Some of the grounds could in principle serve to justify belief or ground knowledge non-inferentially. Religious experience, in particular, is often argued to be a potential ground for properly basic belief. In Evans's view of natural signs, religious belief can be properly basic when based on awareness of a natural sign of God's existence, which needn't involve inferring that God exists from beliefs about the sign.

Let's now turn to the map of defeaters, which can be found in Table 1. I should note that I cannot here list every specific defeater that has been offered. Rather, I will describe various families of defeaters.

Rebutting defeaters aim to provide reason to think that God does not exist. They may defeat partially or fully; if they provide enough evidence that God does not exist to approximately balance out the strength of the evidence in favor of the existence of God, then they will fully defeat the reasons and produce justification defeat and, perhaps, also knowledge defeat (depending on one's view of knowledge).

There are three prominent sorts of rebutting defeaters. The first comes from arguments that the divine attributes are incoherent – either in themselves or in combination. For instance, there are arguments that the notions of omnipotence and omniscience are self-contradictory. There are also arguments that some of the divine attributes are not compossible – for instance that perfect goodness

---

[22] See Ichikawa & Steup (2018), Plantinga (1993), Plantinga (2000), Swinburne (2001), and Swinburne (2005).

[23] See Plantinga (1981) for an early account of Reformed epistemology.

Table 1 Defeaters for belief in God

Defeater type	Defeaters
Rebutting	Incoherence of divine attributes
	Problem of evil
	Problem of divine hiddenness
Undercutting	Objections to the positive grounds
	Superfluity argument
	Problem of unpossessed evidence
Base defeater	Some kinds of genealogical debunking arguments
	Rationalization arguments
Competence defeater	Some kinds of genealogical debunking arguments
	Problem of historical variability
	Problem of disagreement
	Cumulative case argument

precludes freedom.[24] If any of these arguments succeed and the notion of God is incoherent, then there cannot be a God – thus providing a rebutting defeater of belief, reasons, justification, and knowledge. The second is the venerable problem of evil, which comes in many varieties. The basic idea is straightforward: there is much evil in the world, but we should expect God to prevent such evil for, being omnipotent, God has the power to prevent evil, being omniscient, God knows how to use their power to achieve their ends, and being perfectly good, God would want there to be no evil (or a less amount, or no evils of a certain sort). Sometimes instead the problem is stated as a probabilistic comparison of two potential explanations for the evil we see in the world – atheistic naturalism and theism. This version argues that atheistic naturalism better explains and predicts the patterns of evils we see than does theism, and thus the evil we see supports atheistic naturalism over theism.[25] The third, first rigorously presented and popularized by Schellenberg (1993), is the problem of divine hiddenness. In short, given God's goodness and love, we should expect God's existence to be more evident than it is if God really did exist. Thus, we have reason to think that God does not exist from the fact that it is not

---

[24] See Mawson (2018), Oppy (2014), and Swinburne (2016) for recent discussion of these are other puzzles about divine attributes.

[25] See McBrayer & Howard-Snyder (2003), Tooley (2019), and van Inwagen (2008) for a variety of recent discussions regarding the problem of evil. Paul Draper (1989) is notable for defending the latter version.

particularly evident that he does exist.[26] These are not the only rebutting defeaters for the existence of God, but they are the most prominent, widely discussed, and widely accepted.[27]

Undercutting defeaters aim to undercut the force of the grounds supporting belief in God. They broaden the evidential base such that the total, broader base, no longer supports or properly grounds belief that God exists. As with rebutting defeaters, undercutting defeaters can be partial or full and can produce reason, belief, justification, and knowledge defeat. Additionally, some undercutting defeaters may show that the grounds one had for believing that God exists never were good grounds to begin with. In that case, they produce status-revealing defeat.

There are three main types of undercutting defeaters. The first is a very big family, comprised of all responses to the positive grounds for theism that aim to neutralize the force of those grounds. Examples include arguments against the principle of sufficient reason, evolutionary explanations of the appearance of design, and arguments that religious experience has little to no justificatory force. The name for the second undercutting defeater – the Superfluity argument – comes from Van Inwagen (2005), although the objection is much older. Indeed, it was discussed by Aquinas. It goes like this: we can account for all that we see and know about the world at least as well using only naturalistic resources as we can using theistic resources. God's existence and activity are explanatorily superfluous. Thus, explanatory and experiential grounds do not support theism over atheistic naturalism. Testimonial grounds presumably will be epistemically useless if the grounds testified to do not support theism over naturalistic atheism. This argument will presumably overlap somewhat with the first family as individual potential grounds for theism will have to be assessed, but what distinguishes the superfluity argument is that it focuses on undermining the grounds for theism by showing those grounds do not support theism over other explanatory hypotheses.[28] The third is the problem of unpossessed evidence: people have been discussing whether God exists for thousands of years and have written tons evaluating the very grounds had by a typical MMIM believer. Most believers know very little of these discussions. Nobody knows all of them. Surely there's a good chance that there are defeaters lurking in the mass

---

[26] For further discussion, see Howard-Snyder & Moser (2002), Weidner (2021).

[27] For another, see e.g. Everitt's (2004) discussion of arguments from scale.

[28] I take the superfluity argument to be best understood as an undercutting defeater, but some have developed it as a rebutting defeater by adding an Ockham's razor-like principle such as "if the evidence does not favor hypothesis x over y and x includes the existence of an entity e that y does not include, then one should believe the simpler hypothesis y and reject the existence of e." Van Inwagen (2005) offers compelling arguments against such principles. For further discussion, see Thurow (2014a).

of evidence a believer does not possess, and they have no idea whether those defeaters are any good. This evidence of the existence of defeaters itself functions as an undercutting defeater.[29]

Base defeaters can either change the base of one's belief in God to something that is evidently not a good ground for theism, or they can reveal that one's belief in fact is based on different grounds than one thought – grounds that are evidently not good. In the latter case, the base defeater is also a status-revealing defeater, thus defeating belief. In the former case, one's original grounds/ reasons aren't defeated per se; rather, one's doxastic justification and know-ledge are defeated. As far as I am aware there are no standard, widely known base defeaters of the former variety. Individual believers may acquire one when they fall for charismatically presented but evidently faulty reasons. There are, however, several varieties of the latter sort of base defeater.

Certain sorts of genealogical debunking arguments offer one kind of base defeater. These arguments offer evidence for a genealogical account of one's (or a group's) religious beliefs that reveals that the base of religious belief is some process or ground that is plainly not epistemically supportive. Freudian and Marxist explanations of religious belief are good examples. They purport to show that belief in God stems from wish fulfillment, such as a deep need to feel loved by a father figure, or a desire for comfort in a threatening, chaotic world. Today the most plausible genealogical arguments come from the cognitive science of religion (CSR) – a discipline that draws on cognitive science and evolutionary theory to explain religious belief and behavior. Researchers in CSR explain belief in God as either the byproduct of other evolved cognitive traits, or as selected for because of certain benefits individuals or groups get from believing in God. Either way, these real, cognitive/evolutionary explan-ations for belief in God are not reliable indicators of God's existence. The real grounds for human belief are not epistemically supportive. A variety of argu-ments of this sort have been developed in the literature, drawing on various genealogical explanations and epistemic principles (Thurow 2023b). Another sort of argument – rationalization arguments – purport to show that people's stated or apparent grounds for their belief are not their real grounds. Rather, they are mere rationalizations. Rationalization arguments are sometimes combined

---

[29] Ballantyne (2019) offers the most careful defense of this problem, offered for any belief about which there is significant disagreement. Schellenberg (2007) defends a version of this problem for theistic belief. Note that the problem of unpossessed evidence is similar to, although different from, two other problems: the problem of counterfactual interlocutors (possible people who have defeaters), and the Pyrrhonian problem of possible counterarguments (for every positive argu-ment we give, there is somewhere in nature a counterargument that defeats it). See Ballantyne (2019) and Machuca (2011) for discussion of these arguments.

with genealogical accounts of a believer's true grounds, which are then judged to be evidently epistemically poor.[30]

Competence defeaters aim to show that a believer is not competent at evaluating the force of their reasons/evidence/grounds for their belief in God. Competence defeaters aren't reason defeaters, but they can be justification and knowledge defeaters (though see the discussion in Section 2, again, for qualifications). They can also defeat belief as a status-revealing defeater if they show the believer was never competent to begin with.

There are four prominent kinds of competence defeaters for belief in God. First, some genealogical debunking arguments aim to show not that the true genealogy for one's belief in God is rationally defective, but rather that the believer cannot tell whether the true genealogy is not rationally defective.[31] Second, the problem of historical variability notes that if Kristi Christian had been born in India, she'd probably be a Hindu or a Buddhist. If she'd been born in Saudi Arabia she'd probably be Muslim. There are different ways to try to turn this doubtlessly true observation into a defeater for theistic belief. The most plausible, in my view, offers a competence defeater: the lesson to draw from this observation is that humans' cognitive tools and methods for evaluating religious claims are not generally very good and we have no reason to think that our own present tools and methods are any better than any other believer's (or any better than those we would have used had we been born elsewhere in other conditions).[32] Third, there is the venerable problem of disagreement, which also can be developed in various ways. It can be understood as a rebutting defeater: testimonial evidence from people who disagree with us about p who are, as far as we can tell, epistemic peers (i.e. just as intellectually virtuous and well-informed as ourselves) just is evidence for us against p. It can be understood as an undercutting defeater: the fact that so many people who are otherwise epistemically competent come to different views about what the evidence about p supports is evidence that the total evidence doesn't support p (or not-p). This higher-order evidence about the evidence seems to undermine, for those aware of it, whatever support the evidence may have originally given. There are situations and beliefs for which disagreement would, I think, best be understood as defeating in one of these two ways. However, for theistic belief, I think that disagreement is best understood as a competence defeater: widespread disagreement among people who are otherwise epistemically competent demonstrates the class of methods used to form beliefs about God's existence

---

[30] See Leben (2014) and Thurow (2023a).   [31] See Thurow (2018, 2023b).

[32] Thinkers throughout history have reflected on this observation, from Xenophanes to Mill to Kitcher. See Ballantyne (2013), Bogardus (2013), and Kitcher (2015) for contemporary discussions.

are collectively unreliable, and nobody has any reason to think the process they use is more reliable than the others. Somebody may in fact be properly responding to the grounds they possess, but nobody can tell who that is (if anybody is). What is called into question is everybody's competence at evaluating the evidence/grounds – not what those evidence/grounds support. Lastly, all these grounds (as well as others) for generating a competence defeater can be combined into a cumulative case argument.[33]

Ingredients used in one defeater can be used in other defeaters as well. We already observed how disagreement can be used in different sorts of defeaters. Similar things can be said for evil and for historical variability; both can be used to support the problem of divine hiddenness, for example. Furthermore, although multiple defeaters can be combined independently to increase the net strength of defeat, some defeaters can increase in their own strength in combination with another defeater. For instance, a supporting defeater may knock out an objection to, or support a key aspect of the supported defeater. We'll see examples of this in later discussion.[34]

I suggest that most typical MMIM believers will be aware of at least some defeaters on the chart. By "awareness" here I mean de re awareness – that is, they are aware of the phenomena that form the basis of defeaters. They may or may not recognize these phenomena as defeaters. There may be an evaluative epistemic difference between people who merely have a de re awareness of a defeater and those who also recognize the defeater as a defeater (or putative defeater). I won't tease out these subtle epistemic differences here. Mere de re awareness of a defeater is surely sufficient to produce some amount of defeat and in any case many MMIM believers are aware of some of these defeaters as putative defeaters.

Typical MMIM believers are most likely aware of the existence of puzzling instances or amounts of evil, the existence of widespread disagreement by otherwise seemingly rational people, and the tendency of science to explain more and more of reality including, potentially, human religious beliefs. Just as I do not assume MMIM believers could present the grounds supporting their theistic belief in an argument or syllogism, I do not assume they could present these defeaters in an argument or syllogism. Most likely, their awareness of the defeating phenomena is accompanied by felt tension with their theistic belief,

---

[33] This brief presentation of the problem of disagreement as a competence defeater is heavily indebted to Pittard's (2020) Master Argument for Disagreement-Motivated Religious Skepticism. See Benton & Kvanvig (2021) for recent essays on the problem of religious disagreement and De Cruz (2019) for an overview.

[34] Schellenberg (2007), Tersman (2015), Thornhill-Miller & Millican (2015), and Thurow (2023a) illustrate several examples of defeater interaction.

although that tension is surely not always present in their mind and is in most circumstances overwhelmed by their confidence that God exists.

However, MMIM believers who are ignorant of some (or perhaps even all) of the defeaters on the chart may be responsible for their ignorance. If they should have known some of the defeaters, then they will possess a normative defeater – the defeaters they should have known can defeat their theistic belief simply because they should have been aware of those defeaters. What makes it the case that a person should have known something? Goldberg (2018: 160ff) argues that we humans have general epistemic responsibilities to play our social-epistemic roles properly. For instance, a medical doctor is expected to know about the latest professional standards regarding how to treat various conditions. This isn't just a predictive expectation but a normative expectation, for if a doctor is unaware of some relevant professional standard and thus fails to treat a patient's condition in accordance with how that standard recommends, the patient has grounds for complaining and seeking redress. Non-doctors are not expected to know these things. We might predictively expect a particularly well-informed layman to be aware of the professional standards, but if they aren't and we nevertheless take the layman's advice on how to self-treat a condition, we have no grounds for complaining and seeking redress (at least, assuming the layman was simply sharing his honest opinion, was not trying to deceive us, and fulfilled his epistemic duties). There are many kinds of roles that place us under epistemic expectations: professionals, experts, service providers, jobs, and various interpersonal relationships. If I have a social-epistemic role, the proper fulfillment of which would require that I know p, then I ought to know p.

MMIM believers do not in general have professional or expert duties that would require them to be aware of these defeaters. (Some might happen to be professional philosophers of religion; they do have a duty to know these defeaters!) But most – certainly the typical – MMIM believer will be a member of a religious community and religious communities have social-epistemic expectations of their members. At the very least, most religious communities expect their members to know the doctrinal basics of their religion and to have more than a passing familiarity with their authoritative texts. For theistic religions such as Christianity, Judaism, and Islam, fulfilling these expectations would require that one be aware of the problem of evil as their religious texts directly and explicitly address the problem of evil. Members of theistic religions have an obligation to continue to grow in their faith and service to God, which is often taken to require that they come to ever-deeper understanding of God and his will. Acquiring a deep understanding will unveil some of the putative tensions in divine attributes and perhaps the problem of divine hiddenness. Many theistic religions have an evangelistic imperative – they expect their members to be prepared to spread their faith. Effectively carrying out the evangelistic imperative requires some knowledge about the people one might evangelize and some of the obstacles facing their conversion, which surely includes some defeaters (although it may be indefinite which of the defeaters one might need to know).[35]

Many MMIM believers live in a religiously diverse, secular society and they may possess social duties as members of those societies – duties that produce normative expectations to know certain things. Since many diverse secular societies are also democratic, and citizens in democratic societies have social duties to participate in the political process by at least voting, many MMIM believers will have social duties to vote. Voting well requires that one be well-informed about the general features of one's society. Religious diversity is presumably one of those general features. Thus, many MMIM believers will be normatively expected to know about religious diversity, and the problem of disagreement arises right from religious diversity. Some societies include a basic knowledge of religions and their place in society on the state-approved K-12 (or equivalent) school curriculum. People in those societies can be expected to know about religious diversity and the historical variability of religious belief.

In short, many MMIM believers will be aware of at least some putative defeaters on the chart. Many believers will be normatively expected to know about some of the defeaters. Assuming these putative defeaters are genuine (and normative defeat occurs), MMIM believers' belief in God is (at least partially) defeated. Perhaps some MMIM believers manage both to be unaware of any of these defeaters and to lack any normative expectation that they would know of any of them. Their belief in God will not face defeat. However, I suggest (i) few MMIM believers will be in this position, and (ii) many of those who are in this position will very likely one day learn of or acquire a duty to learn of some of these defeaters. And in any case, it would be epistemically sad for theism if the only way to be an epistemically well-off believer is to avoid hearing about or having any duties to hear about the defeaters. Thus we now turn to a new question: are these defeaters any good? If they provide any prima facie defeating force, can they themselves be defeated? The rest of this Element focuses on beginning to answer these questions for a few of the defeaters on the chart.

There are plainly too many defeaters to discuss in the space available to us! Instead, I'll focus mostly on some defeaters that present a threat of justification/ knowledge defeat without requiring an evaluation of the strength of theistic grounds. These sorts of defeaters – including genealogical debunking arguments

---

[35] See, e.g., Bebbington's (1989) definition of evangelicalism as a type of movement within Christianity. For an influential twentieth-century reflection on evangelism, see Newbigin (1989).

and the problem of historical variability – are cleaner defeaters in that, if they work, they defeat theistic belief without having to wade into complicated disputes about the strength of specific theistic grounds. I will not be able to discuss all the defeaters of this sort. For instance, the problem of disagreement will receive only brief discussion here; however, it has its own Element to which I refer the reader for further discussion.[36]

Section 4 will be devoted to making a few comments about the rebutting and undercutting defeaters on the table. Section 5 will discuss the base defeaters, and Section 6 some of the competence defeaters.

4 Rebutting and Undercutting Defeaters

4.1 Comments on Rebutting Defeaters: Divine Attributes, Hiddenness, and Skeptical Theism

Putative incoherence among the divine attributes is very unlikely to produce a defeater for theistic belief. Although theists widely endorse a fairly standard list of divine attributes (e.g. omnipotence, omniscience, perfect goodness, necessary existence, and creator)[37] there are no widely accepted analyses of these attributes. Thus, a demonstration that a specific analysis leads to a contradiction doesn't impugn the attribute itself or show that the notion of God is incoherent. It shows only that *that specific analysis* is problematic. A theist can happily consider another analysis. And since this is philosophy, new analyses will almost assuredly be forthcoming.[38]

In addition, some ways of unifying the attributes give the theist extra flexibility in understanding those attributes. Perfect being theology, which understands God to be the greatest conceivable being, is often used to unify the divine attributes by considering each attribute to be a dimension of greatness or perfection. The greatest conceivable being will presumably have all the perfections in the greatest conceivable combination. If some interpretations of those attributes are self-contradictory, or contradictory in combination with other divine attributes, then presumably those interpretations do not yield the greatest conceivable combination. If an interpretation of the attributes is contradictory, then that interpretation isn't conceivable in the right sense, and so it doesn't provide an adequate understanding of the greatest conceivable being.[39]

To darken the prospects for defeat even more, prominent traditions in the theistic religions say that the divine attributes should not be understood literally

---

[36] See De Cruz (2019).

[37] Other attributes are more controversial, e.g. simplicity and impassibility.

[38] See Oppy (2014) for a similar argument.

[39] See Nagasawa (2017) for a similar argument. See Speaks (2018) for an argument that trying to unify the divine attributes via perfect being theology faces deep difficulties.

to apply to God.[40] Our understanding of the divine attributes – no matter how detailed and technical – are at best analogies or metaphors for the divine nature. Analogies/metaphors do not have to be coherent to be useful as analogies/metaphors. So even if there were genuine contradictions among our best definitions of the divine attributes, no incoherence in God's nature would follow.

Lastly, childhood psychological development indicates that people who come to believe in God tend to begin thinking of God as superknowing, superpowerful, and (perhaps, depending on cultural background) supergood, where "super" vaguely gestures at a level way beyond the human (Barrett 2012). Later theological education tries to tweak and make more precise this conception, but humans tend to fall back on fairly intuitive ways of conceiving of a superknowing, superpowerful, good being; as some scholars put it, humans tend toward "theological incorrectness" (Slone 2004). If this is correct, then the ordinary human concept of God is even more flexible. It isn't committed to any specific analysis of the divine attributes, although presumably some possible analyses surely wouldn't capture the "super" level required (for instance, a theory of God's power that says that God is omnipotent or superpowerful if God can do more than the most skilled human). Even if Zeus and the like don't count as gods by these standards, there is still a lot of conceptual flexibility in how to conceive of God. Incompatibilities among specific analyses of the attributes will not show that God cannot exist.

To be clear: I'm not suggesting that reflecting on how to analyze the divine attributes cannot defeat some people's religious beliefs. Some people may be committed to specific conceptions of God, and finding a contradiction in that conception could defeat their specific set of beliefs about God, spurring a religious crisis, especially for a person who is firmly committed to the defeated conception and has a hard time conceiving of other attractive ways to understand God. What I am saying is that finding contradictions among the divine attributes is not going to defeat belief that God exists. Finding contradictions may defeat the claim that God, understood *this particular way*, exists, but not that God exists. For theists, arguments that certain divine attributes or sets of attributes are incoherent are best seen as puzzles to be resolved by reconceiving the attributes in a way that (a) is coherent, and (b) makes God great enough and as great as can be.

I cannot here say whether and to what extent the problems of evil or divine hiddenness defeat theistic belief. There is considerable dispute about these arguments (really, these families of arguments). However, we can make a couple of useful general observations. First, the interpretive flexibility of the divine attributes may affect the strength of these other rebutting defeaters. The problem of evil does

---

[40] See Williams (2014) for a summary of various medieval Jewish, Christian, and Muslim views.

not typically assume rigorous definitions of omnipotence, omniscience, and moral perfection. Rather, it is understood that anything powerful, knowledgeable, and good enough to count as God could well have prevented, knows about, and presumably opposes, various evils that occur. This is enough to get the problem of evil going. One could respond to the problem of evil by saying that the concept of divine goodness has only the weakest analogical relationship to human goodness and, as a result, we have no reason to think a perfectly good (i.e. divinely good) God would oppose the evils we see. However, this is not a popular response to the problem of evil, perhaps because once divine goodness is understood as very weakly analogous to human goodness, it becomes hard to see God as worthy of worship.[41] So, the interpretive flexibility of the divine attributes does not seem to affect the strength of the problem of evil.

Matters are different with the problem of divine hiddenness. Schellenberg's statements of the problem assert that divine love implies God would be open to a relationship with human persons in such a way that no human person would ever be a nonresistant nonbeliever. Any nonbeliever who does not resist God would be presented with adequate grounds for believing in God. He takes this implication of divine love to be a conceptual truth. Rea argues that moderate views of divine transcendence would call this premise into question, e.g. the view that intrinsic predications of God that "express non-revealed concepts are, at best analogical" (Rea, 2018: 51). Conceptual, a priori reflection on love can only be reliable if the concept of love is non-revealed, but then it is analogical as applied to God. There is nothing particularly surprising in finding that a predicate, which is analogical as applied to God, has implications that fail to apply to God. There may be versions of the problem of hiddenness that do not assume controversial conceptions of divine attributes, but the problem seems less likely to defeat theistic belief due to the interpretive flexibility of divine attributes.[42]

Second, some have argued that the skeptical theist response to the problem of evil, if it works, defeats not just the problem of evil, but many of the positive grounds for theism as well. Evidential versions of the problem of evil observe that there are some evils for which we can see no morally justifying reason (i.e. no reason for allowing it that would be good enough to justify God in allowing it).[43]

---

[41] For arguments against a variety of other attempts to use certain conceptions of being and goodness to get around the problem of evil, see Adams (1999), chapter 4.

[42] Anderson (2017) offers a different reply to the problem of divine hiddenness that is noteworthy in a book on defeaters: she argues that Schellenberg ignores the possibility that nonculpable nonbelief could exist while God provides adequate evidence for God's existence because the nonculpable nonbeliever has defeating evidence for God's existence.

[43] For those who do not like the idea of God having or needing morally justifying reasons, the problem of evil can instead concern whether there are events wherein God does not seem to be good to his creation, as divine love would require (Adams 1999).

Some versions then infer, from this observation, that there is no morally justifying reason for the evils (and thus God doesn't exist because if he did exist he would have, and so there would be, a justifying reason). Skeptical theists question the inference on the grounds that, roughly, (i) we have no good reason for thinking that the possible goods and evils we know of are representative of the possible goods and evils there are, (ii) we have no good reason for thinking that the ways possible goods can justify/not justify possible evils that we are aware of are representative of the ways possible goods can justify/not justify possible evils, and (iii) our knowledge of the history of the universe is so limited that most of the time we cannot tell, for a given evil, which possible justifying goods are present and how they are present, if they are present.[44] Because of (i)–(iii), we have no good reason for thinking that the evils for which we can see no morally justifying reason in fact have no morally justifying reason. For all we can tell, these evils may or may not have morally justifying reasons. And so we are not justified in inferring that they do not have a morally justifying reason.

Some philosophers argue that conditions (i)–(iii) also defeat some grounds for theistic belief, such as the appearance of design.[45] We see the existence of complex humans; they are well-designed to function in their environment. This seems unlikely to have come about on naturalistic views (for the moment we'll just grant this is right and forget about evolutionary explanations because we're interested in identifying a different problem for design grounds for theistic belief). Is it more likely to have come about given theism? Well, how likely is it God would have created complex humans? Skeptical theists can grant that some good things about complex humans are evident: their intelligence, freedom, power, beauty, etc. And they can grant that this would give God a reason to create them. But we cannot infer that God is at all likely to create complex humans because we have no idea whether the goods and evils we are aware of are representative of the goods and evils in existence. For all we know, there is some outweighing evil that would lead God not to create complex humans. Our situation here is parallel to our situation about making inferences from evil. The skeptical theist grants there is a lot bad about the Holocaust, which means there would be something good about it not existing. This gives God a reason to ensure it does not exist. But, according to skeptical theism we can't infer that there is no good reason for allowing it to exist; we have no idea whether there is, and so cannot infer God probably wouldn't allow it.

---

[44] Conditions (i), (ii), and (iii) are paraphrases or similar statements as Bergmann's (2009) ST1–ST4 statements describing skeptical theism.

[45] Bergmann (2009), a skeptical theist, concedes this implication. See also Beaudoin (2005), Maitzen (2007), and Wilks (2013).

Some grounds for believing in God do not depend on expectations of how a good God would behave. Cosmological and moral arguments, for instance, are typically arguments from elimination: there's no other good candidate for explaining why anything contingent exists or why there are moral facts or how we know moral facts. Some religious experiences – particularly vivid mystical experiences, for example – also do not seem undermined. Other more mundane experiences and many apparent experiences of miracles may well be undermined, as their interpretation as having either a divine or merely poorly understood natural source depends on having some view about what God might be aiming to do or communicate with the experiences.[46] Revelation may provide some assistance in interpreting these experiences, but only if belief in revelation itself is justified which, assuming skeptical theism, would have to be based on vivid personal religious experience, testimony to such experiences, or particularly compelling evidence for miracles. Reformed epistemologists can also say that provided the believer holds their belief in normal circumstances in which God intends for humans to form belief, they can know and be justified in believing that God exists. Such a belief needn't be grounded in much – perhaps the reading of scripture or an experience of nature. It's not clear this kind of ground would be defeated by skeptical theism, although well-grounded basic beliefs about a person can be undercut by learning more about that person. Suppose I seem to glimpse Barack Obama in a crowded mall in San Antonio. In some circumstances, this glimpse might ground a justified basic belief that Obama is in the mall. But then I reflect on his possible reasons for being there and I can't think of any that would be particularly plausible – especially since he didn't seem surrounded by an entourage of guards or fawning fans, but he could have good reasons for being there for all I know. That reasonable doubt about whether he would have good reasons to be in the mall seems to undermine, or at least greatly weaken, the justificatory force of the experience since there are potential explanations of my experience, for instance, that it was just someone who looks like him and I've been watching YouTube videos of his speeches so I've got him on my mind. Likewise, if the justificatory force of the Reformed epistemologist's ordinary grounds for theistic belief is more like the force of a glimpse, then doubts about our ability to understand the reasons available to God for doing what he does, together with alternate explanations of our grounds, may together defeat.

Some have argued skeptical theism produces a defeater that leads to a deep form of skepticism. The defeater is this: given skeptical theism, we have no reason to think God isn't systematically deceiving us. Since we have no reason

---

[46] See O'Connor (2013).

to think our knowledge of goods and evils are representative of the goods and evils that could serve to justify God in whatever he does, for all we know there may be goods that deceiving us would achieve, or evils that deceiving us would prevent, that justify God in deceiving us. Typically the mere possibility of us being in a deeply skeptical scenario isn't regarded as a defeater for our beliefs. However, Wilks (2013) argues that, for a skeptical theist, the scenario in which God is a deceiver isn't nearly as epistemically distant as we tend to regard brain-in-a-vat scenarios and Russellian "the world popped into existence just as it is yesterday" scenarios. After all, a skeptical theist believes that God exists, has the power to deceive and, as far as we can tell, may have the will. The proximity of this epistemic possibility, for skeptical theists, seems like it should defeat (at least partially) the default justification we have for trusting our senses.

Various replies to this defeater have been offered. Some insist on a less skeptical theism. Others insist that Moorean commonsense defenses of basic trust in our faculties can resist this defeater.[47] We won't resolve this debate here. Suffice to say that there is a potential concern here that skeptic-minded defenses against various defeaters need to be aware of: the skeptical moves might seep into and undermine positive grounds for theism.

4.2 Undercutting Defeaters

Most undercutting defeaters are aimed at undercutting specific grounds for theistic belief. Each of the grounds mentioned in our description of MMIM believers is the subject of centuries-long debate, some defending the grounds, some offering defeaters for the grounds, others offering defeaters for those defeaters, and so on. We cannot examine any of these defeaters here.[48] Instead, we'll focus on the superfluity argument and the problem of unpossessed evidence, as both defeaters aim to be general and less tedious. They are general in the following sense: they aim to undercut justified belief/knowledge of theism without knocking out the theistic reasons one by one. If they succeed in doing so, they're less tedious: figuring out whether theistic belief is justified/ known will not require us to carefully examine a bunch of grounds and their putative defeaters one by one.

---

[47] For examples of the former, see Cullison (2014), Poston (2014) and for the latter, see Bergmann (2012). For another reply to a variety of excessive-skepticism sorts of objections to skeptical theism, see Rea (2013). Hudson (2020) is a fascinating exploration, in fiction, of these and related issues.

[48] There are Cambridge Elements on many of these grounds for theistic belief. The Stanford Encyclopedia of Philosophy contains excellent overviews of many of them. These contain discussion of several putative defeaters for the grounds. For other useful recent surveys, see Craig & Moreland (2009), Oppy (2006), and Swinburne (2004).

4.2.1 The Superfluity Argument

The superfluity argument aims to undermine the putative force of grounds supporting theism by presenting an alternative explanation of the grounds. The more grounds we can explain naturally, the less overall support is provided for theistic belief by the grounds. Bayesian reasoning can be used to make this argument. According to the relative odds form of Bayes' theorem,

$$\frac{\Pr(T/e)}{\Pr(N/e)} = \frac{\Pr(T)}{\Pr(N)} \times \frac{\Pr(e/T)}{\Pr(e/N)}$$

The ratio on the left compares the posterior probability of the hypotheses T and N in light of evidence e (that is, the probability of the hypotheses given e), the first ratio on the right compares the prior probability of the hypotheses (that is, their probability prior to considering e), and the second ratio on the right compares the likelihoods of the hypotheses (that is, how probable the evidence is on the hypotheses). We can view the various grounds for theism as different bits of evidence e: e1 = various religious experiences, e2 = natural facts that appear well-designed, etc. Let T = theism (roughly, God exists and is the creator of the universe) and N = naturalism (roughly, there is no God or other supernatural beings, but only the entities within nature and laws governing their behavior). A given evidential ground will favor T over N only when the likelihood ratio is greater than 1 – that is, when e is more probable on T than it is on N. Whether T ends up being more likely than N depends of course on the prior probabilities as well, but the change from the prior probability contribution to the posterior probability comes entirely from the likelihood ratio.

We might initially think – and have good reason to think – that a given piece of evidence, e, supports theism. Perhaps e provides some pro tanto evidence in itself (or perhaps in combination with some other information) for theism. However, using a Bayesian approach, e will support T over an alternative hypothesis only if theism better predicts e than the alternative considered. Now the naturalistic defender of the superfluity argument comes along and suggests that naturalism predicts e as well, or perhaps better, than theism. If they are correct, then the likelihood ratio will be less than or equal to 1, which means the evidence does not favor theism over naturalism, and so it cannot suffice as grounds for believing theism over naturalism. Thus, the evidential force of e has been defeated. If the naturalist can pull this off for all the grounds of theism, then a believer will no longer know or be justified in believing that God exists (i.e. justification and knowledge defeat result).

Some believers, depending on their grounds, will have their belief in God at least partially defeated. For example, theists whose grounds include the apparent design of various biological traits. The theory of evolution by natural selection offers a naturalistic explanation for why organisms are well-adapted to their environment. Without this theory, naturalists do not have a great explanation of why organisms are well-adapted, but theists do: God, in his goodness, wants things to live and thrive and so gives them the traits to do so. If e = organisms are well-adapted to their environment, then Pr(e/T) is fairly high and, prior to knowledge of evolution by natural selection, Pr(e/N) is low. The likelihood ratio favors theism (thus, the design argument has some force prior to knowledge of evolution by natural selection). But, once we become aware of evolution by natural selection, we now must examine Pr(e/T&E)/Pr(e/N&E), where E = organisms evolved through natural selection. This ratio looks to be around 1, as now Pr(e/N&E) is fairly high.[49]

At this point defenders of intelligent design will push back, pointing out various biological structures that, they claim, cannot be explained by the present understanding of the theory of evolution (which allows for other explanations of traits aside from natural selection). This isn't a Element about the design argument, so we won't pursue this debate any further.[50] However, even if the defenders of intelligent design are correct that evolution cannot explain some biological traits, it has succeeded in explaining other traits and the general adaptiveness of organisms, so some of the evidential base of the classic design argument has been knocked out. Theists who believed based on that evidential base thus possess partial defeat. Whether this partial defeat amounts to much depends on the strength of their other grounds.

Another ground that is at least partially defeated is evidence in favor of miracles. Consider evidence e = there are many reports of miraculous events – that is, events that cannot as far as we can tell be explained in any naturalistic way and that have some sort of religious significance. This evidence may, assuming the reports come from reliable sources, provide some initial evidence in favor of theism. However, once we consider naturalism's explanatory capabilities, its evidential force is defeated. For, Pr(e/N) is actually pretty high. In any large, complex system of laws and events, many events will occur that, in fact, have a purely naturalistic explanation even though humans have little to no idea what that explanation might be. Surely at least some of those events can be interpreted to have religious significance – as signs of what God wants one to do or as signs of his blessing or judgment. So even if Pr(e/T) is fairly high, so is Pr(e/N) and so the likelihood ratio for this evidence does not favor theism over naturalism.[51]

---

[49] For further discussion of the design argument, focusing especially on likelihood-driven versions of the argument, see Sober (2019).

[50] Pennock (2001) is a useful anthology of texts on intelligent design.

[51] See Thurow (2012) for this point and others about how to understand the force of evidence for miracles in the context of disagreement.

Some evidence about miracles and apparent design is not as easily defeated. Consider e = there are intelligent creatures with the power to reflect on morality and modify their will based on their reflections. $Pr(e/T)$ is arguably a fair bit higher than $Pr(e/N)$ even if we enrich N with the theory of evolution. It is quite unlikely that these sorts of intelligent creatures would have evolved, even on a stable, habitable planet like Earth assuming naturalism, whereas it doesn't seem at all unlikely that there would be such creatures if God exists. So, even if naturalism has an in-principle explanation for the evolution of humans, the likelihood ratio may still favor theism. Thus, e will constitute evidence for theism (and thus will not be defeated by the superfluity argument). Now consider e* = the various events surrounding Jesus's purported resurrection and the testimony concerning it. Although we cannot get into the details of arguments for and against the resurrection of Jesus, we can at least observe an initially strong case to be made that $Pr(e*/T)/Pr(e*/N)$ is much greater than 1, even if we enrich N and T with lots of background information about the Middle East at that time and with various potential explanations of hallucinations and deceptions. These events are the sorts of things you might expect a good God to do, particularly if we assume that this God has interacted with the Jewish people throughout history. But these events are highly unlikely on naturalism, as resurrection of this sort is nearly impossible assuming naturalism, and it seems unlikely that people would honestly and sincerely testify to Jesus's resurrection at great risk to themselves if naturalism were true. It would have been far more likely for people to have just assumed that Jesus was like all the other failed revolutionaries: perhaps inspiring, but still dead.[52]

My intent here is not to endorse this argument for the resurrection. Rather, my intent is to point out that there may well remain cases for individual miracles, provided we have sufficient evidence about the events surrounding the purported miracle, where the likelihood ratio favors theism. And this is so even if naturalism predicts that there will be many reports of miraculous events. A theist's belief grounded on evidence where the likelihood ratio favors theism may not be defeated by the superfluity argument.

There is one more piece of evidence worth noting that seems to resist the superfluity argument: eu = the existence of the universe, where the universe is understood to include all positive contingent facts (including the laws of nature and the initial conditions of the universe). $Pr(eu/T)$ seems fairly high. God doesn't have to create anything, but given his goodness and love, it would not be in the least surprising if he decided to create something to love and care for.

---

[52] See Allison (2021), Craig (1989), McGrew & McGrew (2009), and Swinburne (2003) for detailed examination of the argument for Jesus's resurrection.

Whereas Pr(eu/N) seems really low, as naturalism will tend to treat eu as a brute fact and there is simply no way to predict or explain a brute fact. It's hard to know how likely this brute fact would occur, but it seems quite unlikely, especially if we add to eu the fact that the universe is habitable for life. At any rate, we do not here have a strong case that, with respect to eu, theism is superfluous.

The above set of observations points to a deeper lesson about the superfluity argument: evaluating it will require a careful examination of several different grounds for theistic belief, just as independent evaluation of those grounds requires. So, we don't get a quick route to a defeater here. The superfluity argument helpfully points out that to fully evaluate the evidential force of the various grounds, we need to consider whether alternative, compelling explanations exist for these grounds. But we can't assume naturalism is an all-purpose explainer that will explain away all, or even most theistic grounds. Once again, we will have to examine the grounds one by one to determine the best explanation in each case.

Peter van Inwagen offers a different reply to the superfluity argument. He claims the argument assumes that belief in God is an explanatory hypothesis – that is, that people believe in God because God's existence offers the best explanation of a set of factors that can be presented in "statable reasons or publicly available arguments" (2005: 145).[53] And van Inwagen rejects this assumption. He thinks many of our beliefs – belief in external objects, other minds, that the moon exists, that women are intellectually equal to men, and that God exists – are either hard-wired or are "based on a lot more than what [we are] able to put into words" (2005: 147). So the fact that some alternative hypothesis can explain the statable, publicly available evidence on these propositions tells us nothing about whether our belief in these proposition is justified. Why? Because our belief isn't based on the statable, publicly available reasons. Put in terms of the terminology we've developed here, van Inwagen seems to grant that the superfluity argument might defeat some potential reasons, but he thinks it doesn't defeat propositional or doxastic justification or knowledge because we have no reason to think it defeats our actual grounds.

There are a couple of problems with van Inwagen's reply. I grant that a typical MMIM theist will base their belief in God on more than they can state or make publicly available. Belief in God, much like the belief that your mother loves you, can impact your mind and life in a wide variety of ways. Some of those ways may partially ground your belief even though you can't state them or make

---

[53] Plantinga (2000: 329–31, 370–2, 476–7) also denies that people believe God exists as an explanatory hypothesis and he puts this denial to great work in responding to various potential defeaters for theistic belief.

them publicly available. Many religious experiences are like this, I presume. However, we saw earlier that a typical MMIM believer will ground their belief at least in part on many of the reasons that the superfluity argument attempts to neutralize, such as that the world looks designed, or that there must be an explanation for why the universe exists. Those who aim to debunk religious experiences with naturalistic explanations can run a superfluity argument. If those grounds are explained as well on naturalistic terms as on theistic terms, it does seem that at least some of a typical MMIM theist's reasons are at least partially defeated. If enough are defeated, there could be at least partial justification for defeat and knowledge defeat.

Could van Inwagen grant this point and insist, nevertheless, that not all of a believer's grounds will be touched and so they may well remain justified and have knowledge? I suppose this is possible. Perhaps we are default justified in maintaining our strong beliefs that impinge on our mental life in more ways than we can count, and so we are justified in holding on to these beliefs even if some of our grounds get defeated. But surely there's a limit. Default justification is quite a different matter from a license to maintain no matter what defeating evidence you come across. If all my reasons I can think of – after giving it a lot of thought – are undercut by the superfluity argument, and the remaining reasons I have are likely to be of a type (say, religious experiences) that has generally been undercut, then I have reason to think that my grounds – even the ones I can't quite state – are all (or likely all) undercut. This is itself an undercutting defeater. Whether this defeater is strong enough to completely defeat justification and knowledge will depend on the force of the different defeaters.

Perhaps here van Inwagen will retreat further and say that we don't need any grounds if the belief is hard-wired, it isn't defeated, and hard-wired beliefs can be justified. I see two problems with this response. First, even if belief in God is hardwired, it can (and apparently does) acquire additional justification from reasons such as those mentioned in the above psychological description of a typical MMIM believer. Those reasons can still be defeated even if the belief is hardwired. Second, hardwired beliefs can be defeated too if one were to learn that the process leading to the beliefs being hardwired does not, in some epistemically important sense, track the truth regarding the belief in question and related beliefs.[54] We will examine these kinds of defeaters in Section 5. Many of them argue that we can give naturalistic explanations for why humans believe in God – explanations that imply that human religious beliefs do not track the truth. If the superfluity argument is intended to explain not just

---

[54] Van Inwagen (2009: 133) grants this point. In the same article he raises an objection to an evolutionary debunking argument that we will discuss later.

religious reasons but also religious attitudes, then the superfluity argument includes these sorts of base defeaters. A full evaluation of the superfluity argument would then await an evaluation of these base defeaters.

4.2.2 The Problem of Unpossessed Evidence

The problem of unpossessed evidence points out that the typical MMIM believer (and perhaps even the atypically well-informed believer) is aware of only a small fraction of the evidence regarding God's existence that humanity in total is aware of. Others possess evidence that leads them to different judgments: atheism, agnosticism, or an embrace of different theistic beliefs. And many of these people appear otherwise intellectually competent. Thus, there appears to be a good chance that the evidence a given person does not possess will contain defeaters – that is, will be such that, if the person had possessed it, their belief about God's existence would be defeated. But the fact that there is a good chance such defeaters exist is (once one becomes aware of this fact) itself a defeater for one's belief about God's existence.

There are different ways of analyzing this intuitively compelling argument form. I'll present a modified version of Ballantyne's (2019) Doubtful Fairness version of the argument, as applied to theistic belief. This version captures well the reasoning of the argument. It also closely matches Schellenberg's (2007) subject mode argument for religious skepticism, which is to date the most extensive argument for religious skepticism based on unpossessed evidence.[55]

Here is the argument:

> **Evidence of unrepresentative evidence argument**
> EUE1. If S believes p on the basis of some evidence/grounds E and S has either (i) prima facie reason to disbelieve that E is representative of the total relevant evidence/grounds, or (ii) prima facie reason to suspend judgment whether E is representative of the total relevant evidence/grounds, then S has a prima facie undermining defeater for believing p.
> EUE2. Many MMIM believers believe that God exists on the basis of some evidence/grounds E and have either (i) reason to disbelieve that E is representative of the total relevant evidence/grounds, or (ii) reason to suspend judgment whether E is representative of the total relevant evidence/grounds.
> EUE3. They have no defeater for the undermining defeater for believing that God exists. Therefore,
> EUE4. Many MMIM believers have an undefeated undermining defeater for believing that God exists.

---

[55] Ballantyne (2015, 2019), who has written the most in-depth work on this argument, offers three different versions. Milburn (2023) raises objections to Ballantyne's arguments and develops a fourth version.

The "total relevant evidence/grounds" refers at least to all the evidence or grounds that are relevant to justifying the belief in question that are available to humanity. This would include evidence that one is in some sense aware of but hasn't adequately accounted for, and evidence had by other people that one isn't aware of. Schellenberg's (2007: 23–7) version of this argument also includes undiscovered and undiscoverable evidence: that is, information or facts that nobody in fact is (or could be) aware of, but that would evidentially bear on p, if one were aware of them. A given body of evidence or grounds, E, is representative of the total relevant evidence/grounds, T, with respect to p when (and this is just a stipulation) the doxastic attitude justified by E regarding p approximately matches the doxastic attitude justified by T regarding p. So long as both E and T justify the same general doxastic attitude – belief, disbelief, or suspension of judgment – then E will be representative of T.[56] T and E may justify somewhat different levels of confidence regarding p, and yet E still counts as representative of T. E would be representative of T even if E omits large classes of entirely novel evidence (i.e. evidence very unlike evidence already possessed by the thinker in question), provided the novel evidence wouldn't, taken as a whole, affect which general doxastic attitude was justified.

Premise EUE1 says that if you believe p and have reason to think that your grounds for your belief are not representative of the total evidence (or you have reason to suspend judgment about its representativeness), then you have an undermining defeater for believing p. This principle plausibly explains many examples. Suppose Joe sees, for the first time, a can of Coke and notices that it is a red can. He then notices that all Coke cans in the package are red. He has some evidence that all Coke cans are red. But this evidence doesn't justify belief that all Coke cans are red. After all, his sample of evidence is quite narrow. For all he knows, cans in other towns, states, or countries are given different colors. And he doesn't have any evidence of the color of cans anywhere else. Joe has reason to suspend judgment about whether his evidence is representative, and he is not justified in believing that all Coke cans are red. It is easy to construct similar examples (e.g. concerning attributing intentions to people and explaining physical phenomena that are not directly observable). Ballantyne (2019: 173) offers another familiar example: ten years ago you did some research on an economic issue (say, whether minimum wage increases lead to job loss), and you came to

---

[56] Alternative notions of "representativeness" have other requirements (e.g. that all the significant evidential sources in T for p are sampled in appropriate balance in E). The notion I've stipulated, which closely follows Ballantyne's notion, works for our purposes because it can be used in EUE1 to present a sufficient condition for a form of defeat. The additional requirements mentioned in alternative notions of representativeness (such as the example mentioned above) can be relevant if evidence that those requirements are not met is evidence that E is not representative in my and Ballantyne's sense.

a fairly firm belief. But you haven't had time to keep up on the issue for the last several years. You now decide to investigate it once again and you find, after doing a literature search online, that hundreds of books and articles potentially relevant to this issue have been published since you last examined the issue. And a cursory glance through them reveals many of them argue against, or present evidence that raises doubts about, your belief about this issue. You haven't had the chance to look carefully through any of this, and yet it seems already you should suspend judgment. Why? You have good reason to suspect that your evidence is not representative. For all you can tell, this new evidence may contain something that would tell against your belief.

Often we have no reason to doubt whether our evidence is representative. For instance, when I judge someone's shirt to be red. I have every reason to trust my own perceptual faculties and no reason to think anybody else's experiences would provide any contrary evidence. I have no reason to think or even suspect that I'm hallucinating or that the lighting is odd.

Premise EUE2 seems quite plausible. Many MMIM believers may be aware, in general terms, of much of the evidence regarding God's existence that humanity has discussed – cosmological reasons, design reasons, religious experience, evil, etc. However, they are aware that there is considerable discussion and dispute about these reasons. They may know about some of these disputes, but they know (or can easily discover) that there are many objections to the various reasons that they simply haven't considered. Many MMIM believers are also aware that many people embrace quite different religious beliefs (or reject religious beliefs entirely) and that these people have their reasons. They may not know what those reasons are, but they have good reason to think those reasons exist and have some chance of being good reasons. Some Theravada Buddhists have enlightenment experiences that seem to them to reveal that selves are nothing and that ultimate reality is nirvana – a state of undifferentiated bliss. Some MMIM believers may be aware of these experiences, others may not – but they know that Buddhists have some grounds for their beliefs. And finally, many MMIM believers know that atheists and agnostics have their reasons and offer naturalistic accounts to explain the evidence we see. They may not know much about the details of these accounts, but they know the accounts exist and that there is some chance those accounts undercut positive reasons for theism.

What about EUE3? For EUE3 to be false, MMIM believers would need some reason to think that the reasons/grounds that they have – despite being limited in the ways just mentioned – are nevertheless representative. That is, they'd need some ground for thinking that all the other reasons they are unaware of will likely not make a difference as to whether their belief that God exists is justified.

As far as I can see, there might be two kinds of grounds of this sort. First, the grounds they have are so strong that it is unlikely any other set of reasons would be strong enough to undermine them. Second, they have reason to think that someone else has surveyed the reasons they are unaware of and, according to the surveyor, those reasons don't make a difference. Can MMIM believers have either of these sorts of reasons?

Plantinga famously defends the first sort of move (albeit in reply to other defeaters). He motivates it with an example involving memory.[57] Imagine George applies for a fellowship and bribes a colleague to write an inaccurate recommendation letter inflating his qualifications. The colleague refuses and writes a letter to the department chair informing them of George's inappropriate request. However, the letter goes missing and another colleague reports seeing George trying to enter the colleague's office through a window. In fact, George did not attempt to enter the colleague's office; indeed, he made no attempt to intercept the letter. He clearly remembers what he was doing that day: he was hiking by himself in the mountains. A third person – say, the department chair – may well be justified in believing George attempted to steal the letter. Even if the chair initially had some reason to trust George, the circumstantial evidence undermines those reasons in this case and provides the chair with good reason to doubt George's testimony that he was out hiking by himself. However, George himself remains justified in believing he didn't attempt to steal the letter. He clearly remembers being out hiking by himself. He can recognize that the circumstantial evidence gives some reason for thinking he stole the letter, but this evidence is nowhere near strong enough to defeat the justification he has from his clear memory of having been out hiking by himself. Thus we see the following lesson: potential defeaters may fail to defeat a person's belief if their belief is grounded in a sufficiently epistemically solid way.

We could apply this lesson to the evidence of unrepresentative evidence argument. Suppose George has reason to think there is evidence about his potential guilt that he does not possess: he hears there are other testifiers, he's sure his past unsavory request has left further traces he can't recall, and the university has requisitioned his computer. No matter. He still clearly recalls hiking alone in the mountains on the day in question. His memory is a sufficiently strong ground to give him reason to think that (just about) any evidence that he was not out hiking alone is faulty. His memory (or his memory experience, depending on how to understand the epistemology of memory) is itself a defeater–defeater for the unpossessed evidence. Surely the defeating evidence could mount so high that eventually memory is unable to function as

---

a defeater–defeater, such as if "the letter turns up in [George's] back pocket; [his] fingerprints are all over the file it was kept in; the mountain [he] thought [he] was hiking on that afternoon was destroyed by a volcanic eruption the preceding morning" (Plantinga 2000: 372n8). But absent such strong evidence undermining his assumption that his memory has been functioning properly, memory can serve as a defeater–defeater for unpossessed evidence.

Plantinga suggests that a person's belief in God could be grounded in religious experience, or in the proper functioning of the human mind's *sensus divinitatis* (in response to the prompting of the Holy Spirit), and that these grounds could serve as defeater–defeaters just as memory does in George's case.[58] So even if the believer is aware that there is relevant evidence they do not possess, if their belief is grounded as indicated by Plantinga, they have a defeater–defeater for the evidence of unpossessed evidence. EUE3 is false for such a believer.

This reply is, in one way, plausible. The problem of unpossessed evidence seems especially challenging when we investigate issues that cannot be resolved by direct observation or experience. I can't see microscopic particles, or the insides of stars, or the distant past or future. For complicated systems, I often can't just discern the right or best way to organize that system. For these issues, we gain knowledge by gathering indirect evidence and then working out the best explanation/account of that evidence. Learning there is unpossessed evidence for these issues is like learning the puzzle you're working on is missing many pieces: you have good reason to doubt you're putting it together well. But for matters that can be resolved by direct observation (or memory of direct observation), we are rightly less concerned about unpossessed evidence because the fact that we can (apparently) directly tell that p is true indicates to us that the unpossessed evidence will likely make no difference to whether p is true and whether I am justified. If some people can just tell that God exists, through religious experience or through whatever is involved in the *sensus divinitatis*, then they can thereby know clearly – "see" almost – that God exists and have good reason to think that the unpossessed evidence will likely make no differ-ence to whether God exists and whether they are justified.

However, as Plantinga grants, we can acquire defeaters even in cases where we can apparently just directly tell that p. And some of our faculties are more vulnerable to certain kinds of defeat in this way than others. For instance, although George's memory of having been walking alone on the mountain isn't defeated by the circumstantial evidence mentioned in the example above, it is more easily defeated by those with contrary memories of the same event. Suppose Steve seems just as clearly to remember walking the same path on the mountain

---

[58] See Plantinga (2015: 121), where he makes this sort of reply to the problem of evil.

that day, at the same time, and not seeing evidence of anyone else. Think, more generally, of how easy it is for our apparent memory of past events to be defeated by others' (who we have decent reason to trust) apparent memory of the same events. We might initially have reason to trust ourselves over others, but with enough evidence from others whom we have reason to trust, defeat comes quickly. This is especially so when there are plausible explanations for why we might have falsely seemed to have remembered p.

Grounding for belief in God may be similarly vulnerable to defeat. Many people apparently have radically different religious experiences; many Buddhists claim to experience fundamental reality as qualityless. Other people lack experiences at all, despite apparent openness to God. And, as we'll see, there are plausible explanations for why it might clearly seem to people that God exists.

However, if all this defeating evidence were unpossessed by a theist, Plantinga's argument plausibly diagnoses such a theist's epistemic state. Their religious experiences or the proper functioning of their *sensus divinitatus* gives them apparent direct awareness that God exists. That apparent awareness is reason to think their evidence is representative. However, once they acquire the above defeating evidence, they have decent reason to doubt that they are directly aware of God. Once in that state, the problem of unpossessed evidence arises. Here we see how two defeaters can work together: defeat for the claim that one is directly aware of God's existence enables the defeater from unpossessed evidence to become operational.

Let's turn to the second potential ground for rejecting EUE3: reason to think that someone else who has reliably surveyed the relevant evidence judges that it wouldn't make a difference to one's epistemic state. A typical MMIM believer will have at least two reasons of this sort. First, typical MMIM believers are embedded in extended religious communities that typically contain scholars or priests who have a fairly good grasp of the relevant evidence. A typical MMIM believer may not personally know such a scholar or priest, but they will usually have good reason to think that their community contains such people.

One might doubt whether there are any religious experts who are aware of all the relevant evidence. If by "all" we mean, literally, all arguments and evidence ever presented, then there are no religious experts. But we don't need super experts like these in order to justifiably think that the evidence has been surveyed adequately. So long as the experts are aware of a sizable sampling of the evidence – including the supportive and potentially defeating evidence – then they can have reason to think they have adequately sampled the evidence. Furthermore, this work may be divided among many experts. Perhaps some are experts about the problem of evil, others are experts about various evidence for theism and defeaters of that evidence, others about other religions and defeaters that may come from awareness of other religions, and so on. So long as a MMIM believer has reason to believe that there are religious experts in his community who have collectively adequately sampled the relevant evidence and who judge the potential defeaters that arise as not making a difference to one's epistemic state, he has reason to think that his grounds are representative, and that EUE3 is false.

Some kinds of defeating evidence can, in principle, knock out this reply. For instance, if the MMIM believer becomes justified in believing that the problem of religious disagreement undercuts the rationality of relying on the religious experts in his community, then he will no longer have this sort of reason for thinking that his grounds are representative. And then the defeating strength of the problem of unpossessed evidence will be restored. Once again, we see that two defeaters can work together: the defeater from religious disagreement enables the defeater from unpossessed evidence to become operational.

A typical MMIM believer will have another reason to think his grounds are representative: he has grounds for thinking not just that God exists, but that God, an omniscient being, has revealed God's existence to humanity. God, being omniscient, knows all the relevant evidence; God is the greatest conceivable cognitive expert. So, the MMIM believer's grounds for believing in God are rooted in testimony from the most reliable possible testifier who is aware of all (actual and potential) defeating evidence. And clearly – because God is testifying to God's existence – none of the evidence unpossessed by God's audience makes a difference epistemically to their belief. A person whose belief is grounded in testimony from the greatest conceivable cognitive expert on all matters thus has every reason to think their grounds are representative (and thus that EUE3 is false).

This reply might seem to be viciously circular, for doesn't the unpossessed evidence call into question the evidential force of the very evidence that grounds the MMIM believer's belief that God, an omniscient being, has revealed Godself? No, the reply is not viciously circular; unpossessed evidence doesn't undercut by undermining the source of the evidence, E, one presently has regarding p; rather, it provides evidence that it is inscrutable what the total body of evidence, including E and much one does not possess, indicates regarding p. That E provides evidence for p isn't undermined. So, if E provides not just evidence that p, but also evidence that one's evidence is representative, E can both support p and deflect the potential defeat coming from evidence of unpossessed evidence. The following analogy illustrates this point. Steve visits a library and sees shelves upon shelves of books on the life of Abraham Lincoln. He glances through a few books and sees that there is disagreement among authors on the nature of Lincoln's relationship with his wife. Now imagine two possible ways Steve's research could go. First, suppose he reads one book which tells a certain story about their relationship; the story is coherent and intrinsically plausible and the author provides evidence for the story, but the book gives no reason to think this version of the story is better than any others that Steve knows exists in the library. Here, the unpossessed evidence defeats. Second, suppose instead he reads a different book that describes their relationship the same as the first book did; however, this book also contains information about the author's mastery of scholarship on Lincoln (there's a brief biography describing her training and laurels and there are copious footnotes demonstrating her awareness and understanding of a vast expanse of Lincoln scholarship). Here, the unpossessed evidence doesn't defeat. Why? In both cases, the same story is told of Lincoln, and good support is given for that story. In both cases, Steve is aware of unpossessed evidence. The difference is that in the second case, the evidence Steve happens across also provides evidence for its representativeness. And note: the evidence for the story about Lincoln and the evidence for the representativeness of the evidence come from the very same source. The MMIM believer is in a similar circumstance: his evidence that God exists comes from a source that also provides evidence of representativeness – namely, evidence that God has revealed Godself.

There is a potential way to defeat this reply: acquire evidence that God has not revealed Godself or that one has reason to think that the source for belief in revelation isn't reliable. As with the potential defeaters for the other replies, unpossessed evidence would thus provide a defeater only if accompanied by another set of defeating evidence. So these three replies all teach us the same lesson: the problem of unpossessed evidence does not itself provide a defeater for a MMIM believer's belief in God. However, unpossessed evidence regarding God's existence isn't thus rendered completely inert. It can be activated as a defeater, but only if accompanied by other evidence that defeats the above replies. Unpossessed evidence can thus, at most, function as what we might call a *supplemental defeater*. In the next two sections, we'll examine defeaters aimed at undermining the sources believers employ to form and maintain theistic belief. If those defeaters succeed, unpossessed evidence will then become an active supplemental defeater. If those defeaters fail, unpossessed evidence will remain inert (unless and until some other defeater emerges that can knock out the above replies).

5 Base Defeaters

In this section, we're going to focus on two prominent sorts of base defeaters for theistic belief: a family of genealogical debunking arguments, and rationalization arguments. Both arguments aim to show that theistic belief in fact is based on grounds (or processes) that are different than believers expect, simply based on first-person reflection on the grounds of their belief. And the real grounds for theistic belief are epistemically defective. Thus if these base defeaters work, they defeat theistic belief via status-revealing defeat. That is, they show that theistic belief lacked some important epistemic status (knowledge, justification) all along.

5.1 Genealogical Debunking Arguments

Pascal Boyer, anthropologist and prominent scholar in the CSR, writes in his book, *Religion Explained*, "everybody seems to have some intuition about the origins of religion. Indeed, anthropologists and psychologists . . . constantly run into people who think that they already have a perfectly adequate solution to the problem" (Boyer, 2001: 5). Religious beliefs are ubiquitous in human societies throughout history. There must be some explanation for why humans hold religious attitudes. Perhaps unsurprisingly, people think they know the explanation. Theists need some explanation for why others reject their specific religious beliefs. Atheists and the nonreligious need an explanation for why the bulk of humanity takes gods so seriously. Everyone wants to see themselves as rational and correct and thus those who disagree as mistaken. So they have incentive to find an explanation for why others hold religious beliefs that will also explain why they have come to mistaken beliefs. Often those explanations, if true, posit an epistemic defect.

Fortunately, today we can do better than offer armchair intuitive explanations for other folks' religious attitudes. Drawing on evolutionary theory, cognitive psychology, anthropology, and the history of religions, scholars have developed several testable theories that have received empirical confirmation. It's safe to say that none are developed well-enough or are well-enough supported to merit outright belief. But they show promise.

These scientific theories of religious attitudes are naturalistic. That is, they present explanations that do not appeal to any nonnatural factors, such as the intentions and actions of God. These naturalistic explanations, as we shall see, call into question whether religious beliefs are reliable/justified/known, for the explanations imply humans would be led to religious beliefs regardless of whether God (or other religious entities) exist.

These naturalistic explanations appeal to processes that believers do not attribute to themselves, processes that appear rationally dubious. Thus these explanations potentially pose a threat of base defeat. We must now ask: does this widespread attempt to explain religious beliefs present a defeater for those beliefs – theistic belief, in particular?

To answer this question, we first need a survey of the most plausible natural-istic explanations for theistic belief. We only have space for a very brief and partial survey.[59] Today cognitive-evolutionary explanations are dominant. These explanations suggest that theistic belief was either adaptive, the byprod-uct of other adaptive traits, or an exaptation – that is, it emerged as a byproduct and then became adaptive.

According to byproduct explanations, various adaptive human cognitive features make it very easy to acquire, or even bias humans toward, religious beliefs. Preparatory explanations (a subspecies of byproduct explanations) do not explain the origin of theistic belief, but explain why humans are able to entertain and find attractive thoughts about God. These preparatory explan-ations include the following features: (i) god concepts are minimally counterin-tuitive, (ii) humans are intuitive dualists, (iii) humans have an intuitive theory of mind, and (iv) childhood development of the theory of mind has children expecting people to be superknowers.

Minimally counterintuitive concepts take a natural[60] human concept (such as *tree*) and vary at most a couple core features of the concept (e.g. *invisible tree*). God concepts involve minor variations on the concept of a person – namely, it is a concept of an invisible and highly powerful and knowledgeable person. Minimally counterintuitive concepts spread easily because they are unexpected, fairly easy to comprehend, and sometimes (as with god concepts) offer useful resources for explaining events in the world.

"Theory of mind" is a phrase that denotes the natural human cognitive ability to conceive and understand agents as possessing and being influenced by beliefs, motives, concerns, and goals. The theory of mind operates separately from our intuitive theory of biology. As a result, as Paul Bloom (2005) has argued, humans are intuitive dualists and thus they can easily conceive and think about gods as persons with minds but not bodies. In addition, young children think of persons as hyperknowers – that is, as knowing what is knowable or worth knowing. Thus they easily maintain the idea that God is a hyperknower even as they learn that other humans are far more limited knowers.

The above features all prepare the human mind to entertain and take seriously the idea of a god. Perhaps this is all that is needed to explain theistic belief since human creativity would almost assuredly lead humans to entertain the idea of

---

[59] For more detailed surveys see Norenzayan (2013), Stausberg (2009), and White (2021). The survey that follows is a compressed version of (and uses some of the phrasing from) my survey in Thurow (2023b: 293–7).

[60] I take a natural concept to be one that human communities will typically acquire through their interaction with their environment, employing their maturationally natural abilities (McCauley 2011 develops the concept *maturationally natural*).

gods. However, other byproduct theories take a further step and suggest factors that nudge humans toward, or select for, belief in gods. Barrett (2004) has famously argued that humans possess a hypersensitive agency detection device (HADD) that is set to interpret ambiguous information as evidence of the activity of an agent. Barrett thinks HADD was an evolutionary adaptation, but as a byproduct it will leave humans suspecting there is an agent at work in many situations where they can find no other direct evidence of an agent's activity. They will thus be inclined to think there are invisible agents at work, such as spirits, ghosts, and gods.

Deborah Kelemen and her colleagues have conducted various studies that indicate that humans – children, especially – engage in promiscuously teleological thinking. That is, "they reveal a strong tendency to see purpose in nature and generally prefer purpose-based (i.e. teleological) over mechanistic physical explanations as early as preschool, and they generate these types of explanations even when they have not heard them or had them reinforced by others" (Kundert & Edman 2017: 76). These tendencies are shown even in adults when they are made to perform experimental tasks under cognitive load (i.e. quickly, or while performing other tasks, or with distractions). As a result, Kelemen suggests that humans are intuitive theists – that is, they have a default proclivity to see entities as intentionally caused by god(s).

Some scholars have argued that some religious beliefs, including belief in big gods – Norenzayan's (2013) concept of gods that are superpowerful, superknowing, and morally concerned – are adaptive. These scholars tend to accept the insights of the byproduct accounts, and so tend to view theistic belief as an exaptation. These adaptationist/exaptationist views regard religious beliefs as adaptive because of how they enable humans to thrive in a social environment.

Norenzayan's (2013) exaptationist explanation states that belief in big gods is adaptive because big gods concepts are tools that large societies came upon to solve the puzzle of big groups.[61] The puzzle is that the survival of big groups requires a high level of social cooperation, but once groups get too big other mechanisms of rooting out free riders are not effective (e.g. kin selection, reputation management, and reciprocity) and so big groups should fall apart. People who believe in big gods and can find ways of reliably identifying other true believers will benefit from strong cooperation because they believe god is watching and will enforce good behavior. In principle, such believers can construct large societies.

---

[61] For a different adaptationist explanation, see the divine punishment theory of Johnson & Bering (2009) and Bering (2011).

Based on naturalistic evolutionary theories of religion such as these, John Wilkins and Paul Griffiths (2012) defend an influential base defeater debunking argument for theistic belief. In summary form, the argument goes as follows:

1. *Causal premise.* Our evolutionary history explains why we have the religious beliefs that we have (including belief in God).
2. *Epistemic premise.* Evolution is not a truth-tracking process with respect to religious truth.
3. *Metareligious assumption.* Objectivism/realism is the correct account of religious discourse regarding the existence and characteristics of religiously significant entities such as God. Therefore,

C. *Theistic skepticism.* Human belief that God exists is not justified.[62]

The causal premise is intended to be justified by the various evolutionary theories mentioned above. We'll grant that the evidence is strong enough to support the claim that one of these theories (or some suitable development of one of them) is likely to be true. The metareligious assumption assumes realism about key parts of religious discourse, especially regarding the sentence "God exists". This sentence is to be interpreted as asserting that God is an objective, mind-independent being. This is clearly how the sentence has been historically understood. This assumption is present to prevent an avenue of escape from the conclusion (namely, by embracing non-realism about the discourse).

The epistemic premise has been supported a couple of different ways. Wilkins and Griffiths argue that evolution is not truth-tracking because it is not sensitive to the truth – that is, the causal evolutionary process operates regardless of what the religious facts may be and receives no signals about the religious facts to use in leading a species to religious beliefs. It's not a process that can discriminate the truth, whatever the religious truth may be. Braddock (2016) directs attention to the outputs of the evolved mechanisms posited to explain religious belief: they are highly diverse and mostly false! For the explanations of theistic belief can also explain a wide range of other religious beliefs, including belief in polytheistic pantheons and various finite gods and spirits; most of these beliefs are false. Since the outputs of the mechanism are mostly false, the evolved mechanism does not track the truth.[63] A hidden epistemic assumption of the argument is that if

---

[62] This is constructed from their numbered-premise argument regarding evaluative skepticism, substituting relevant changes to produce religious skepticism (as they clearly intend these arguments to be parallel). See Wilkins & Griffiths (2012: 142–3).

[63] Braddock is concerned with reliability rather than truth tracking (although the former is one way of interpreting the latter). Also, he argues for the more humble claim that we should suspend judgment about whether the evolved mechanism is reliable.

a belief-forming/sustaining process is not truth-tracking (or, if one justifiably believes it is not truth-tracking), then one is not justified in holding beliefs resulting from that process.

I think this debunking argument goes wrong at both the causal premise and the epistemic premise. Take the latter first. Whether a process tracks the truth is to be determined relative to a set of conditions in which the process is fit to operate. These conditions surely include the conditions in which the process evolved. Suppose now that God created humans with the intent that they would come to believe in God (or some sort of supernatural presence) through the evolutionary processes in question. In that case, the conditions in which the process is fit to operate include the existence of God, and so the process would track the truth regarding God's existence. So, whether the evolutionary process is truth tracking with respect to the belief that God exists depends exactly on whether God exists. The epistemic premise cannot be established without first arguing that God does not exist or would not use the evolutionary process to generate belief in God.

Braddock's argument seems solid when evaluating whether the process tracks the truth with respect to specific beliefs about specific deities. However, the process could still be reliable for the general belief that there is a divine being of some sort. Other belief-forming processes we have are like this, for example, memory and perceptual-based counting of large collections of objects (especially when they are moving around). Our memory of details can often be quite wrong while we are accurate about general facts. Many people who witness the same event may have quite different accounts of the details while agreeing about some generalities about the event. Braddock grants this reply, but points out that if this is the best that can be said in response, belief in traditional theism stands defeated (2016: 279).

This brings us to the causal premise and what I take to be a deeper problem with the debunking argument. It is vulnerable to what I call the Religious Reasons Reply which, in short, observes that for all this debunking argument says, theists may well have grounds that in fact justify belief in God. The cognitive-evolutionary explanations provided by these theories do not completely explain an individual's belief in God. They also do not explain religious systems of belief, that is Christianity, Judaism, Islam, and monotheistic Hinduism. These beliefs carry for more content than the cognitive-evolutionary mechanisms can explain. At most, those mechanisms can explain why humans in general have a cognitively default disposition to take seriously various claims about invisible agents, including gods. Other beliefs and experiences are necessary to direct this disposition at a specific target religious entity. And as we've seen, a typical MMIM has a range of experiences and beliefs that will direct them toward a specific religious entity.

Religious experiences, various sorts of religious reasons (such as cosmological reasons), and testimony all help explain why and how a person holds their belief in God. This fuller explanation for individual beliefs in God includes what may well be good reasons.[64] Even granting that the cognitive-evolutionary mechanisms described by these theories are not truth-tracking, it doesn't follow that the fuller explanation of a person's belief in God – which includes what may well be good reasons – isn't truth-tracking. Thus, Wilkins and Griffiths' debunking argument does not show that people's belief in God is explained by a non-truth-tracking mechanism that is other than what they would expect. At most, the argument shows that a non-truth-tracking mechanism helps explain religious belief. This does not suffice to defeat belief in God.

5.2 Rationalization Arguments

Rationalization arguments raise suspicion that the reasons people present for their belief in God do not match the real explanation for why they believe in God. We seem prone to rationalization, so why not think we rationalize our religious beliefs as well? Indeed, rationalization might be a natural result of the confirmation bias: we tend to hunt out and endorse reasons that appear to support our beliefs and reject or ignore reasons that question them. The reasons we cling to in this way may not be our *real* reasons – the explanation, that is – for why we hold our belief. Rather, they may be more like clothing we put on to look good in certain situations.

Scholars have defined "rationalization" in many ways; here, for our purposes, we'll work with a slightly modified version of Audi's (1993: 415) definition:

> A first-person rationalization, by S, of S's belief that p (call it B) at t, is a purported account of B, given by S, which (a) offers one or more reasons, R, for B, (b) represents the belief as prima facie rational given R; but where (c) R does not explain why S believes p at t.

Beliefs that are rationalized with reasons R – in the sense indicated by Audi's definition – thus are not in fact held on the basis of R. Thus, no matter how strong the R reasons are for believing p, R can play no role in rendering S's belief doxastically justified (or known). Appealing to R – again, no matter how good R is – does nothing to justify B or to ward away potential defeaters for B. If R includes what in fact are very good reasons for believing p, then S's belief that p may well be propositionally justified (and so in some sense S ought to believe what in fact she believes). However, supposing S's grounds for her belief in fact

---

[64] For further reflections on the Religious Reasons Reply, see Thurow (2013, 2014b, 2018, 2023a, 2023b).

do not have what it takes to render B justified or known, then S's actual belief is doxastically unjustified. She shouldn't (epistemically) hold it in the way that she does, even though she should hold the belief on different grounds (namely R).

The religious reasons reply to Wilkins and Griffiths' debunking argument will thus be undercut if the religious reasons mentioned in the reply in fact are rationalizations. And this is precisely what Derek Leben has argued. Leben suggests that if an unreliable psychological mechanism M better predicts S's belief B than does R (a purported account of B, given by S), then it is more likely that M causes B and R is a rationalization than that R causes B.[65] He then claims that psychological mechanisms such as those mentioned in the cognitive-evolutionary explanations of belief in God described above better predict belief in God because it predicts a wide range of religious beliefs in various gods and the religious reasons typically marched out by theists are simply too weak to explain why theists hold those beliefs.

However, as the religious reasons reply observes, those mechanisms do not predict any specific religious beliefs. They predict at most an inclination for humans to take seriously concepts of invisible (or hard to find) beings that have certain kinds of characteristics. But which concepts? That depends on their exposure to concepts. And for most believers, their exposure to the concepts they take seriously will include exposure to reasons such as those that characterize a typical MMIM believer. Furthermore, humans readily reject the existence of some of these beings. Nobody believes in Zeus anymore. No adult believes in Santa or the Tooth Fairy. What explains why we reject these entities? Arguably, reasons of various kinds. If reasons can explain why we come to reject some of these beings, we should also expect reasons to explain why people come to accept others. Lastly, many of the proposed psychological mechanisms would predict that people take seriously several god concepts – that is, it predicts that societies would tend to be polytheistic. That is a sound prediction; most societies in human history have embraced polytheism. However, some people and societies have embraced ethical monotheism (i.e. belief in one God that is concerned with ethical human behavior). Adaptive or exaptive theories predict that people who come to embrace ethical monotheism – especially if they can reliably identify others who also embrace it – will have an adaptive advantage, and so the belief will spread. But these theories do not explain how humans manage to get themselves to embrace ethical monotheism in the first place. Exposure to reasons such as those that characterize a typical MMIM believer plausibly play a role in explaining why people embrace ethical monotheism.

---

[65] This sentence is modified from Thurow (2014b: 199). Leben does not explicitly state this principle, but it is an accurate summary of the debunking conditions he describes in (2014: 345).

Leben is surely correct that some religious reasons plausibly cannot explain why people believe in God, such as the ontological argument. It's too abstract and controversial – even amongst theists themselves. But others are taken seriously enough that it is question-begging in this context to assume the reasons are too poor to persuade. Cosmological reasons, design reasons, religious experiences, and experiences of miracles are all taken very seriously by a wide range of religious traditions. And, of course, religious people – as they do in other areas of life – rely on testimony from perceived experts.

The base defeaters considered in this section fail to defeat theistic belief. At most, they show that belief in God is often influenced by factors believers ordinarily wouldn't take to be causes of their beliefs. But we have not seen any good reason for thinking that religious reasons of the sort mentioned in my description of MMIM believers are not truly grounds for a typical MMIM believer's belief.

Although these sorts of debunking arguments fail to present a defeater for theistic belief, other sorts of debunking arguments show more promise. We turn to these in the next section.

6 Competence Defeaters

Competence defeaters of theistic belief aim to show that a believer is not competent at evaluating the force of their reasons/evidence/grounds for their belief in God. They are not reason defeaters – that is, one's reasons are not shown to be defective as reasons or grounds. Hypoxia offers a classic example of competence defeat.[66] Those suffering from hypoxia – a lack of sufficient oxygen supply to the body's tissues – can suffer from impaired judgment wherein deeply flawed reasoning will, on the contrary, seem evident. If you have reason to think you are suffering from hypoxia, you have a competence defeater for other kinds of reasoning you perform, such as in math problems. You should not trust your judgment based on reasoning; beliefs formed when in the presence of evidence of hypoxia are not justified or known. Of course, it is possible, while possessing evidence you are suffering from hypoxia, that in fact you are not suffering from hypoxia and in fact have reasoned flawlessly (or despite suffering from hypoxia, you in fact have reasoned flawlessly in this case) – the defeat doesn't indicate that your reasons are flawed. Rather, it undermines your rational confidence in your ability to rationally respond to reasons.

In this section, we'll build up to a cumulative case competence defeater for theism. We'll begin with genealogical debunking arguments and then build to

---

[66] Lasonen-Aarnio (2012) discusses this example.

the cumulative case defeater by adding considerations from historical variability and disagreement.

6.1 Another Genealogical Debunking Argument

Instead of taking plausible genealogical explanations of theistic belief to show that theistic belief is grounded other than it appears and that its actual grounding is epistemically defective, we could take those explanations to rationally undermine the confidence that a theist should have in her competence at making judgments about the existence of God.

Let's revisit the base debunking argument from the last section. We saw there is reason to doubt the epistemic premise of that argument, which says that evolution is not a truth-tracking process regarding religious truth. For if God exists and created humans to be open to spiritual realities using the cognitive-evolutionary mechanisms described earlier, then the process would be truth-tracking. We'd have to have reason to reject this scenario before we would be justified in believing the epistemic premise (and no reason was given to reject this scenario).

Granting all of this, something still appears epistemically worrisome. On this account of theistic belief, people would believe that God exists via these cognitive-evolutionary mechanisms regardless of whether God exists. If God didn't exist and humans had evolved to have these mechanisms, they'd likely still believe that God exists. Something about this kind of insensitivity seems problematic. We can explain why as follows. Suppose a theist who has some grounds for their belief comes to have some reason to doubt that God exists from, say, the problem of evil. Now, God's existence and God's nonexistence are both live epistemic possibilities for this theist. How are they to judge which to believe? Now, given the insensitivity of the process that generates and sustains belief in God, we should be epistemically concerned. For it would do no good to appeal to the grounds of this process, for such grounds do not evidentially distinguish between the scenarios in which God exists and uses the process, and the scenario in which God does not exist and evolution guides us to these mechanisms.

Here's another way of putting the point: I can't tell whether I'm competent in believing that God exists without using the process I have in fact used when coming to believe in God. And that process may or may not be competent: if God exists, it is; if God doesn't, it isn't. I have at least some reason to doubt that he does. In this circumstance, I can't do anything to counter that reason to doubt, for just using the process can't discriminate between the case in which God exists and the case in which he doesn't. In both cases, I use the same process to arrive at and vindicate my belief. Since that process doesn't evidentially distinguish the two cases, my justification is defeated.

An analogy may help support this point. In the film, *Total Recall*, Douglas Quaid purchases a "virtual vacation" to Mars through the Rekall company. The company hooks the "vacationer" up to a machine and implants in them a bunch of false memories of having gone on a vacation. However, just as the machine is about to be activated, Quaid disconnects himself from it – or so it seems – believing he is a secret agent whose cover will be blown. He then goes on (or appears to go on) a series of adventures that take him to Mars. At the end of the film, he wonders whether all of his adventures really happened, or whether they are implanted vacation memories.[67]

Quaid has some reason to think the machine may have implanted memories into him. If it did, he wouldn't be competent in trusting his memories regarding these events. If it didn't, he would be competent in relying on these memories. But he can't tell which it is. The memories themselves don't distinguish between the case in which his memories were implanted and the case in which they weren't. It seems clearly irrational for him to appeal to his memories (no matter how vivid) to justify his belief that he went to Mars. He is not justified in believing (and does not know) that he went to Mars.[68] A typical theist whose belief is formed just using the cognitive-evolutionary mechanisms mentioned by the genealogical theories and who knows about the problem of evil seems to be in an analogous epistemic situation to Quaid.

This debunking argument offers a competence defeater for belief in God and it evades some of the objections to the base debunking argument. However, it remains vulnerable to the religious reasons reply. Just as Quaid could be justified in believing he went to Mars if he had other reasons, such as photos and the testimony of others that they saw him there, so a theist could remain justified if they had other reasons supporting their belief in God.

6.2 Cumulative Case Competence Defeater

Now that we've moved to a competence defeater, an avenue for response to the religious reasons reply opens up: granting that MMIM theists tend to have reasons, are there reasons to doubt their competence at assessing those reasons? Yes. There seem to be many reasons for doubt.[69]

---

[67] I discuss this example further in Thurow (2018).

[68] This is where level-splitters will quibble. They'll say that if in fact Quaid wasn't implanted with false memories, then if he goes ahead and trusts his memory, he'll have a reliable, safe, and competent belief and so will know. I just register that, to me, this view seems clearly false. But even if one embraces it, one needs to explain how it is that Quaid's believing is somehow rationally flawed (even if he knows).

[69] This argument is inspired by King (2016), although our list of considerations differ somewhat, and he seems to view it as an undercutting defeater, whereas I see it as a competence defeater. The names for C1–C3 come from King and my descriptions of them are paraphrases (sometimes

C1: *Something's Wrong with Most of Us*. Billions of people around the world and throughout history have religious beliefs. Many of these beliefs are incompatible with others and at most one religious system is entirely correct. Most religious beliefs are false and thus those who have false beliefs either have misleading grounds or have assessed non-misleading grounds incorrectly. And yet very many religious believers are intelligent and well-meaning (King 2016: 134).

C2. *Difficulty in Assessment*. Many religious grounds/reasons are difficult to assess, such as the ontological argument, various cosmological arguments, the problem of evil, and cumulative case arguments such as arguments from miracles (which require a fair amount of knowledge about history and potential explanations, and involve difficult comparative assessments of strength). Prominent religious thinkers, including Aquinas and Pascal, have noted this observation (King 2016: 136).[70]

C3. *Disagreement about Assessment*. Very many intelligent and well-meaning people disagree about the force of the various religious grounds/reasons (King 2016: 137).

C4. *Historical Variability*. People's religious beliefs tend to line up with where and when they were born. And people come to hold their beliefs in similar ways: they're raised in a specific religion (or in a place where that religion has some cultural cachet) and receive testimony from people around them. This testimony is reinforced with prayer and rituals and personal religious experiences. Some of these personal religious experiences may be generated through a process of "spiritual kindling" that can generate experiences of spiritual powers for people from a wide range of spiritual traditions (Luhrmann 2020). The religious truth is supposed to be the same everywhere and everywhen, and yet most religious beliefs are false. So these common methods are not reliable in general.[71]

C5. *Epistemically Distorting Influences*. Various factors influence peoples' religious beliefs in a way that likely distorts their ability to accurately respond to the supporting force of their grounds for belief. For example, the confirmation bias leads people to interpret evidence in a way that supports their belief and to ignore or downplay contrary evidence. Humans want to see themselves as rational, and so are inclined to view themselves that way regardless of the reasons they possess on a given issue. Humans engage in motivated reasoning: they tend to interpret evidence in a way that protects their social identity.

---

with expansions) of his descriptions. My C4 is similar in spirit to his C5 (although it has an entirely different name and description). His C4 is basically the problem of unpossessed evidence, which I think does not present a competence defeater. His argument does not include the epistemically distorting influences I describe in C5.

[70] See Aquinas SCG I.4–5 and a quote from Pascal cited in King (2016).

[71] Law's (2018) X-claim argument against belief in hidden beings focuses on many of these observations.

Some religious believers are subject to sheltering or indoctrination. Theists tend to love God and loving someone can distort one's assessment of evidence regarding their character (Thurow 2023a).[72]

Not all the considerations mentioned in C1–C5 will apply to every theist, but many will apply to many theists, including MMIM theists. Some of these considerations may, on further reflection, turn out to not have much force. But the sheer number of considerations, combined with the fact that they offer several independent grounds for a lack of competence, make an initially strong case that at least some of these considerations are likely to be genuine, thus defeating the theist's belief that they are competent, thus defeating their belief in God.

Suppose the cumulative case competence defeater is genuine and undefeated. What follows? First, the defeater would appear to undermine our competence in evaluating the arguments against God's existence as much as the grounds for God's existence. Thus this competence defeater would defeat rebutting defeaters and – for similar reasons – undercutting defeaters for belief in God. Suspension of judgment regarding God's existence seems to be where this defeater takes us. Second, as with arguments from disagreement, this defeater would appear to corrode a lot more than theistic belief. Many political, moral, and philosophical beliefs are also vulnerable to this defeater. A Moorean modus tollens is much less plausible as a response to this defeater than it is to arguments for general skepticism. It just isn't as intuitively clear that beliefs targeted by C1–C5 (and their analogues for politics, morals, and philosophy) are known or justified in these circumstances. And philosophers tend to take these sorts of defeaters a lot more seriously than they do general skeptical arguments (see, e.g. Ballantyne 2019, Brennan 2010). That said, this competence defeater for theistic belief is in some ways more threatening than similar arguments regarding moral, political, and philosophical beliefs. Some moral, political, and philosophical beliefs will survive this defeater, whereas it is far from clear that any religious beliefs will survive.[73] In addition, some moral and political propositions that, when understood abstractly, would be defeated, plausibly would survive defeat when particularized to specific communities. For instance, "democracy is the best form of government" may not survive the defeater, but "democracy is the best form of government for us here in Texas" may. Similar moves cannot be given for religious claims such as theism; "God exists" cannot be defeated while "God exists for us here in Texas" is undefeated (for the same person in the same circumstances) as the latter entails the former.

---

[72] For further considerations, see Smith's list of "cognitive lubricants for religious attributions" (2017: 183ff).

[73] When "religious belief" here is understood to be directed toward propositions that make predications of religious entities like gods, spirits, qualityless Brahman, Nirvana, and the like.

6.3 Replies

Although the competence defeater has rarely been presented in this cumulative way, different parts of this defeater have been extensively discussed in the literature on disagreement, the argument from historical variability, and debunking arguments. One advantage of combining these separate arguments into the cumulative case argument is that we are better able to see that these are all different ways of questioning competence and the replies that are offered to individual arguments have broader significance for all the grounds for questioning competence.

In this section, I survey these replies. Unfortunately, I cannot evaluate all of them fully; as you'll see, there are too many for that here. They're also challenging to evaluate because they are tied up with difficult epistemological issues that are just now coming into clear focus. The cumulative case competence defeater is, to my mind, the most challenging defeater for belief in God, but also the most challenging to satisfactorily evaluate. I think the variety of replies shows that it is far from clear that the cumulative case defeater is a genuine defeater, but matters are complicated and each of these replies deserves more careful examination.

A good response to this defeater will require the theist to have some grounds that justify them in maintaining confidence in their competence despite the evidence of C1–C5. Many philosophers have argued for a restriction on what kinds of grounds can do the job: the grounds must be dispute independent. That is, if a putative ground is called into question by the defeater, then that ground cannot serve to justify confidence in one's competence.[74] This independence requirement would, if true, severely hamper the theist. It's not clear what dispute-independent facts a typical theist could appeal to. That they are smarter than those who disagree? Not likely; most MMIM are average and there are exceptionally smart people with various religious views. That their religious tradition has greater intellectual depth and has wrestled more extensively with challenges? This might rule out some religious claims; but many others are grounded in deep and rich traditions (e.g. Christianity, Islam, Judaism, Buddhism, and various forms of Hinduism). Other responses are equally unpromising. As will be clear, perhaps unsurprisingly, most responses to this defeater reject the independence requirement. And, indeed, it is controversial even outside of religious contexts.[75] (This is the first and perhaps most important epistemological issue tied up with proper evaluation of this defeater.) Now, on to the replies.

---

[74] David Christensen is the most prominent defended of an independence requirement. See Christensen (2014) and references therein.

[75] For a recent careful and insightful evaluation of the independence requirement both on its own and as it is used in disagreement arguments regarding belief in God, see Pittard (2020).

Self-defeat. This argument eats itself. C1 applies to those who would accept this defeater and embrace agnosticism or atheism for those are also positions regarding religion that conflict with many other positions, so they would need reason to think they are competent in evaluating this defeater. C2 and C3 apply as well – the cumulative case competence defeater is difficult to assess and there is disagreement over how to assess it. C4 is also true regarding agnostics and atheists. C5 may be less applicable to those evaluating this defeater; some distorting influences won't apply. But others will (e.g. confirmation bias, bias to see oneself as rational). So, if this defeater succeeds in defeating religious belief, it would also seem to defeat belief that the defeater is a good defeater. If it defeats itself in this way, what threat could it be to belief in God?[76]

Themes from Reformed Epistemology. Many of the things that Plantinga says in defense of his Reformed epistemology seem not to help much in response to this defeater. He says that a theist can be doxastically justified (in a deontological sense) in holding their belief provided they are not epistemically irresponsible and surely some theists will think the defeater through carefully and conclude they're still justified. They aren't flouting any epistemic duties (Plantinga 2000: 178). But according to this defeater, they would be flouting an epistemic duty: a duty to account for evidence of their incompetence. Plantinga accuses several objections to theism of assuming (incorrectly) that people believe in God as a hypothesis meant to explain data.[77] It's clear this defeater makes no such assumption. Externalism about warrant/knowledge doesn't help either. This defeater can grant that some people really do have what it takes to know – they believe competently or function properly in maintaining their belief (at least, before becoming aware of the defeater). The problem is that, given C1–C5, nobody can tell if they're competent and they know most people are not competent. Upon learning that information, it seems one is not justified in maintaining their beliefs – even if they happened to be one of the lucky competent ones prior to learning of the defeater.

However, Plantinga's memory case analogy – which we discussed earlier in the section on the problem of unpossessed evidence – is more promising. Just as someone who has what strikes them as a very clear memory that p may justifiably continue in their belief that p despite knowing others believe differently, so someone who has what strikes them as a clear experiential awareness of God's presence may justifiably continue in that belief despite knowing others believe differently. Indeed, they could grant much of C1–C5 and say, "and yet, despite all that, I see God's presence clearly." Their clear experience of God's presence

---

[76] The self-defeat response is perhaps the earliest response to competence defeaters like this. See e.g. Plantinga (2000: 428, 446). See Pittard (2020) and Matheson (2015) for recent discussions.

[77] For example Plantinga (2000: 91f).

would provide evidence of their competence, and thus evidence that those who have come to other conclusions must have made a mistake.[78]

Even if this response is sound, there is a question of how often theists have the right sort of experience (or adequate memory of such an experience). Many theists have doubts alongside their religious experiences and traditions such as Christianity admit that religious experiences can be misleading and so need to be examined. Various discernment methods have been developed.[79] In later work, Plantinga seems to grant that many believers will often not be in a position to know in this way that God exists (2015: 67).

Affective Rationalism. John Pittard (2020) argues that the independence requirement can justifiably be violated when one has rational insight into matters that bear on the truth of the proposition in question. Some believers may have rational insight into the strength of various grounds supporting theism. These insights needn't be easily expressible in an argument. Those with such insight successfully rationally discern that certain grounds support theism and it will strongly seem to them that they so discern. They have reason to think they are competent at discerning the grounds they do discern. Pittard adds that affective responses such as emotions may deliver moral, axiological, or aesthetic insights that better enable a believer to assess theism. For instance, they may have affective insight into the value of various states of affairs, the value of God's properties, and the value of the character, teachings, and works of religious figures. Some of God's properties and their value – such as holiness – may only be properly graspable through an affectively mediated religious experience. These theists' insight and awareness of their insight give them reason to think they are competent. Pittard grants that theists will sometimes have unclear insights or reason to doubt that they have rational insight and that in such cases they have some evidence of incompetence and their credence in theism should decrease, although depending on the case it may remain fairly high.

Rich Testimony.[80] Theists, including MMIM believers, are typically embedded in a community of believers and the community plays multiple important roles in explaining, supporting, maintaining, spreading, and embodying the beliefs of the community. A Christian, say, is aware that people with different religious beliefs also have communities that play similar roles for them. However, a Christian will typically have very little evidence about how those communities function, whereas she will have extensive evidence about her own community. She'll have multiple lines of evidence in support of the reliability of

---

[78] See Frances (2008) for an interesting challenge to this move. His argument would also, if sound, make problems for Moser's epistemology discussed below. One way out is to acknowledge that other factors mentioned here also contribute to justifying confidence in one's competence.

[79] See, e.g. Willard (2012).   [80] See Thurow (2023a) and a related argument in Greco (2010).

people in her community. She'll have rich testimony in favor of her belief in Christianity – namely, testimony that her belief is true and that there are good reasons for her belief from people she has an excellent reason to trust. When the community contains rich testimony that G are good grounds for theism and a believer in the community herself also finds G plausible on her own, then she has reason to think that she and her community are competent. She has not nearly as much reason for thinking so about other religious communities and their members. She will have some reason to think that other communities may have rich testimony that supports their beliefs, but her evidence for that is far less than her evidence that her own community has rich testimony. This is some reason for her to favor herself and her own community as competent. Combine rich testimony with rational insight into grounds for theism and strong religious experiences, and a believer may have strong reason to think they are competent.

Benign Circularity. Moon (2021) argues that some theists have deflectors for this defeater – where a deflector prevents a defeater from ever functioning as a defeater for a person who has the deflector – because (assuming their belief in God and other religious beliefs are initially justified) they have justification for thinking that they have formed their belief competently and others have formed their beliefs incompetently. For instance, a Christian will have reason to think that her belief is competently formed because it was formed in the way that Christianity says God works to produce belief in her, namely, by believing based on testimony from the Church, reading the Bible, and seeking God's presence in prayer (Moon calls this a self-promoting proposition). Furthermore, those who haven't relied on this process are not using a competent process for coming to see that God exists (Moon calls this an others-demoting proposition). So, she is justified in regarding her belief in God as competently formed and justified in thinking that others' religious beliefs that do not rely on this process are not competently formed. These justified beliefs deflect the competence defeater – it never becomes a defeater; it is prevented from becoming a defeater for the Christian who is justified in believing both the self-promoting and others-demoting propositions. This deflector is based on religious beliefs that are party to disagreement, but Moon argues that this sort of circularity is benign. Relying on our methods to justify belief in the competence of our use of those methods, to avoid skepticism, must be benign – unless and until one acquires excellent reason to reject a method. But the Christian never gets excellent reason to reject their method. Their method has provided justified beliefs that deflect this potential defeater.

Moon's argument highlights a feature of religious beliefs that we also mentioned when discussing the problem of unpossessed evidence: religions have not just metaphysical views about the nature of reality (including God), but also epistemological views about how humans know religious claims about reality. Their epistemological views can provide resources for defeating or evading potential defeaters. Indeed, the epistemological views of religions make it quite difficult to follow the independence requirement.[81] A Theravada Buddhist, for instance, will say that following the independence requirement is bound to lead to error because humans are so bound to appearances and belief in the enduring self that the only way to escape these illusions is through an enlightenment experience, which can only be achieved after extensive preparation. To attempt to follow the independence requirement, then, in trying to decide whether to accept Buddhism is tantamount to simply rejecting Buddhism. It is thus impossible to follow the independence requirement: to follow it would require taking a stance that is part of the dispute. The same goes for Christianity. Paul writes, "Where is the one who is wise? ... Where is the debater of this age? Has not God made foolish the wisdom of the world? For since, in the wisdom of God, the world did not know God through wisdom, God decided, through the foolishness of our proclamation, to save those who believe" (1Cor 1:20–21). He continues, "When I came to you ... my speech and my proclamation were made not with persuasive words of wisdom but with a demonstration of the Spirit and of power, so that your faith might rest not on human wisdom but on the power of God" (1Cor 2:1,4–5). Following the independence requirement doesn't sound like resting on a demonstration of the Spirit. Many theologians, including Aquinas, say that knowledge of God comes through trust in God's word as conveyed through the Church and through "tasting and seeing" (Ps 34:8) that God is good through prayer, contemplation, and participation in the sacraments. Following the independence requirement would have us abandon these methods. Since it is impossible to follow the independence requirement and it seems there ought to be some way of rationally pursuing a response to this defeater, circular ways that violate the requirement ought to be taken seriously.

The Transformative Gift. Moser's epistemology of theistic belief, constructed through deep engagement with texts like the above from the Pauline corpus (as well as other Biblical texts) embodies and builds on many of the ideas already mentioned.[82] Moser is explicit that epistemology of theism should be built on an understanding of God's nature. Since God is perfectly good and loving, God would be most interested in motivating humans, cooperatively, to believe in God in a way that transforms them from selfishness into ever-closer approximations of Jesus's sacrificial love. God wouldn't force himself on humans to coerce them into transformation, so we shouldn't expect him to make his reality readily known. Rather, God will offer a transformative gift to those who are

---

[81] Pittard (2014) and Pittard (2020: 247ff) make similar arguments.   [82] Moser (2010, 2017).

open to God's spirit. The transformative gift is an experiential encounter with God, through the Holy Spirit, in which one is authoritatively convicted in conscience and forgiven by God of sin and thereby called into volitional fellowship with God in perfect love and into rightful worship of God. Based on this experience one is transformed by God from default tendencies to selfishness and despair to a new volitional center with a default position of unselfish love, including forgiveness, toward all people and of hope in the triumph of good over evil by God. One's experience of the gift and one's concomitant incremental moral transformation are evidence of God's existence.

If Moser's epistemology is correct, then once again it would be a big mistake to follow the independence requirement. That would be exactly the wrong way to try to find God. Furthermore, it isn't remotely surprising, on this view, that many people throughout history are incompetent at finding the religious reality.[83] Unless one opens oneself up to God's spirit, one has no reliable way to find God. That said, Moser thinks people from other religious traditions may well be offered the transformative gift. The gift is an encounter with God, although God isn't necessarily presented as part of the propositional content of the experience. God is encountered de re. The experience is evidence for God's existence, but because of the person's religious background, they may interpret its import differently.

Moser's epistemological account arguably embodies benign circularity. Moser says he has received the transformative gift. He thereby has evidence that God exists, but that evidence only comes through openness to God's grace. Many people lack that evidence and indeed come to varying religious beliefs. But they provide no defeater for Moser's belief because, given what he has come to justifiably believe through the transformative gift, they're all using the wrong methods. They're not appropriately open to God's grace. However, some have encountered the transformative gift and have been transformed. They have and present evidence for the rest of us of God's existence, even if they themselves don't quite see it or interpret that evidence differently.

The Pragmatic Turn. Pascal famously accepts that humans are simply incompetent at determining the nature of reality and the ultimate fate of humanity. One might accept the sad epistemic implications of the competence defeater but offer something else in replacement for justified belief in God: namely, non-doxastic attitudes such as commitment to or acceptance of God's existence.

---

[83] King (2016) uses Bayesian reasoning to argue that if a theistic view predicts the evidence of incompetence, then that evidence needn't disconfirm belief in God much. I think his argument treats the evidence as a rebutting or undercutting defeater. However, if the evidence constitutes a competence defeater, then one should regard as inscrutable some of the quantities in the Bayesian calculation.

There are different ways of justifying this pragmatic turn. Like Pascal, one might offer decision-theoretic reasons to commit to God's existence. Otherwise, one might suggest that the great stakes of potentially missing out on an eternal relationship with an infinitely good God lower the standards for rationality. Perhaps, so long as the proposition that God exists is in the evidential ballpark – it's something like a "live option" in James's sense, it is rational to at least accept that God exists.[84]

As mentioned earlier, we don't have the space to adequately evaluate these responses. But our discussion reveals, I think, at least this: it is far from clear that the cumulative case competence defeater defeats belief in God for MMIM believers. These varied responses show promise and each of their resources is available to MMIM believers. That said, most MMIM believers will, over the course of their lives, have some substantial doubts about the rationality of their belief in God. This nearly universal phenomenological fact offers some decent reason to believe that believers' grounds aren't strong enough to be fully resistant to serious grounds for doubt. Even if there are good replies to the competence defeater, it is (it seems to me) the most serious ground for doubt about believers' competence that we have examined. Likely, then, it at least partially defeats belief in God for typical MMIM believers (that is, their degree of confidence in theism should decrease somewhat after acquiring the competence defeater). Further evidence for this claim: imagine you were to learn that C1–C5 are in fact all false. There's been a massive conspiracy about them which has just been uncovered. In fact, most people share the same religious beliefs and Big Psych has been deceiving us in trying to get us to feel down on our intellectual competencies. In this imaginary situation, it seems like theists' confidence in theism should go up! That indicates that C1–C5 at least partially defeat.

How far should a theist's confidence decrease? That's very hard to say. It depends on the strength of the above replies. It depends on the strength of the theist's grounds. It depends on whether those grounds are defeated by the problem of evil or by rebutting and undercutting defeaters narrowly targeted at various grounds. If, accounting for all of these grounds and defeaters, theistic belief should decrease substantially, then the problem of unpossessed evidence will be unleashed and ramp up the level of defeat. But if the grounds for theistic belief in fact are strong and MMIM theists see as much, and the other defeaters don't have much force, and these replies to the competence defeater have substantial force, then perhaps the justification for a typical MMIM

---

[84] Pace (2011) defends this sort of argument. See Pittard (2020: 282ff) for a recent challenge to the pragmatic turn.

believer's belief ought only decrease slightly. Then, the problem of unpossessed evidence remains chained.

There is no clear and easy general defeater for a MMIM believer's theistic belief. If my reasoning here is correct, whether their belief is justified depends more on the strength of their positive grounds and the force of more targeted rebutting and undercutting defeaters.

References

Adams, Marilyn McCord. (1999). *Horrendous Evils and the Goodness of God*, Ithaca, Cornell University Press.

Allison, Dale. (2021). *The Resurrection of Jesus: Apologetics, Polemics, History*, New York, Bloomsbury.

Alston, William. (1991). *Perceiving God*, Ithaca, Cornell University Press.

Anderson, Charity. (2017). "Divine Hiddenness: Defeated Evidence," *Royal Institute of Philosophy Supplement* 81: 119–32.

Audi, Robert. (1993). "Rationalization and Rationality," in *The Structure of Justification*, Cambridge, Cambridge University Press, 405–30.

Baker-Hytch, Max & Matthew Benton. (2015). "Defeatism Defeated," *Philosophical Perspectives* 29: 40–66.

Ballantyne, Nathan. (2012). *Born Believers: The Science of Children's Religious Belief*, New York, Free Press.

   (2013). "The Problem of Historical Variability," in Diego Machuca, ed., *Disagreement and Skepticism*, New York, Routledge, pp. 239–59.

   (2015). "The Significance of Unpossessed Evidence," *Philosophical Quarterly* 65(260): 315–35.

   (2019). *Knowing Our Limits*, New York, Oxford University Press.

Barrett, Justin. (2004). *Why Would Anyone Believe in God?* Walnut Creek: AltaMira Press.

Beaudoin, John. (2005). "Skepticism and the Skeptical Theist," *Faith and Philosophy* 22(1): 42–56.

Bebbington, David. (1989). *Evangelicalism in Modern Britain: A History from the 1730s to the 1980s*, London, Unwin Hyman.

Beddor, Bob. (2015). "Process Reliabilism's Troubles with Defeat," *The Philosophical Quarterly* 65(259): 145–59.

   (2021). "Reasons for Reliabilism," in Jessica Brown & Mona Simion, eds., *Reasons, Justification, and Defeat*, Oxford, Oxford University Press, pp. 146–76.

Benton, Matthew & Jonathan Kvanvig. (2021). *Religious Disagreement & Pluralism*, Oxford, Oxford University Press.

Bergmann, Michael. (2005). "Defeaters and Higher-Level Requirements," *The Philosophical Quarterly* 55: 419–36.

   (2009). "Skeptical Theism and the Problem of Evil," in Thomas Flint & Michael Rea, eds., *Oxford Handbook of Philosophical Theology*, Oxford, Oxford University Press, pp. 375–99.

(2012). "Commonsense Skeptical Theism," in Kelly James Clark and Michael Rea, eds., *Reason, Metaphysics, and Mind*, Oxford, Oxford University Press, pp. 9–30.

Bloom, Paul. (2005). *Descartes' Baby*, Cambridge, MA, Basic Books.

Bogardus, Tomas. (2013). "The Problem of Contingency for Religious Belief," *Faith and Philosophy* 30(4): 371–92.

Braddock, Matthew. (2016). "Debunking Arguments and the Cognitive Science of Religion," *Theology and Science* 14(3): 268–87.

Brennan, Jason. (2010). "Scepticism about Philosophy," *Ratio* 23: 1–16.

Chandler, Jake. (2013). "Defeat Reconsidered," *Analysis* 73.1: 49–51.

Christensen, David. (2010). "Higher-order Evidence," *Philosophy and Phenomenological Research* 81(1): 185–215.

(2014). "Disagreement and Public Controversy," in Jennifer Lackey, ed., *Essays in Colllective Epistemology*, New York, Oxford University Press, pp. 142–63.

(2022). "Epistemic Akrasia: No Apology Required," *Nous* (online first): 1–22.

Conee, Earl & Richard Feldman. (2004). *Evidentialism*, Oxford, Oxford University Press.

Craig, William Lane. (1989). *Assessing the New Testament Evidence for the Historicity of the Resurrection of Jesus*, New York, Edwin Mellen Press.

Craig, William Lane & J. P. Moreland. (2009). *The Blackwell Companion to Natural Theology*, Malden, Wiley-Blackwell.

Cullison, Andrew. (2014). "Two New Versions of Skeptical Theism," in Trent Dougherty & Justin McBrayer, eds., *Skeptical Theism: New Essays*, New York, Oxford University Press, pp. 250–63.

De Cruz, Helen. (2019). *Religious Disagreement*, Cambridge, Cambridge University Press.

Donagan, Alan. (1999). "Philosophy and the Possibility of Religious Orthodoxy," in *Reflections on Philosophy and Religion*, ed. Anthony Perovich, New York, Oxford University Press, pp. 3–13.

Draper, Paul. (1989). "Pain and Pleasure: An Evidential Problem for Theists," *Nous* 23(3): 331–50.

Everitt, Nicholas. (2004). *The Non-existence of God*, New York, Routledge.

Frances, Bryan. (2008). "Spirituality, Expertise, and Philosophers," *Oxford Studies in Philosophy of Religion* 1: 44–81.

Gibbons, John. (2006). "Access Externalism," *Mind* 115: 19–39.

Goldberg, Sanford. (2018). *To the Best of Our Knowledge: Social Expectations and Epistemic Normativity*, Oxford, Oxford University Press.

(2021). "The Normativity of Knowledge and the Scope and Sources of Defeat," in Jessica Brown & Mona Simion, eds., *Reasons, Justification, and Defeat*, Oxford, Oxford University Press, pp. 18–38.

Goldman, Alvin. (1979). "What is Justified Belief?" in G. Pappas (ed.), *Justification and Knowledge*,

Dordrecht, Reidel, pp. 143–64.

Greco, John. (2010). "Religious Knowledge in the Context of Conflicting Testimony," *Proceedings of the American Catholic Philosophical Association* 82: 61–76.

Graham, Peter & Jack Lyons. (2021). "The Structure of Defeat," in Jessica Brown & Mona Simion, eds., *Reasons, Justification, and Defeat*, Oxford, Oxford University Press, pp. 39–68.

Hardy, Alister. (1979). *The Spiritual Nature of Man*, Oxford, Oxford University Press.

Horowitz, Sophie. (2014). "Epistemic Akrasia," *Nous* 48(4): 718–44.

Howard-Snyder, Daniel & Paul Moser. (2002). *Divine Hiddenness: New Essays*, Cambridge, Cambridge University Press.

Hudson, Hud. (2020). *A Grotesque in the Garden*, 2nd ed., Grand Rapids, Eerdmans.

Ichikawa, Jonathan Jenkins & Matthias Steup. (2018). "The Analysis of Knowledge," *Stanford Encyclopedia of Philosophy*, Edward N. Zalta (ed.), https://plato.stanford.edu/archives/sum2018/entries/knowledge-analysis/.

James, William. (2002/1902). *The Varieties of Religious Experience*, New York, Modern Library.

King, Nathan. (2016). "Religious Skepticism and Higher-Order Evidence," *Oxford Studies in Philosophy of Religion* 7: 126–56.

(2021). *The Excellent Mind*, New York, Oxford University Press.

Kitcher, Philip. (2015). *Life After Faith: The Case for Secular Humanism*, New Haven, Yale University Press.

Kornblith, Hilary. (1983). "Justified Belief and Epistemically Responsible Action," *The Philosophical Review* 92(1): 33–48.

Kundert, Corey & Edman, R. O. (2017). "Promiscuous Teleology: From Childhood Through Adulthood and from West to East," in Hornbeck, R., Barrett J., & Kang M., eds., *Religious Cognition in China*, Switzerland, Springer, pp. 79–96.

Lackey, Jennifer. (1999). "Testimonial Knowledge and Transmission," *The Philosophical Quarterly* 49: 471–90.

Lasonen-Aarnio, Maria. (2010). "Unreasonable Knowledge," *Philosophical Perspectives* 24(1): 1–21.

(2012). "Higher-Order Evidence and the Limits of Defeat," *Philosophy and Phenomenological Research* 88(2): 314–45.

(2021). "Dispositional Evaluation and Defeat," in Jessica Brown & Mona Simion, eds., *Reasons, Justification, and Defeat*, Oxford, Oxford University Press, pp. 93–115.

Law, Stephen. (2018). "The X-claim Argument Against Religious Belief," *Religious Studies* 54: 15–35.

Leben, Derek. (2014). "When Psychology Undermines Belief," *Philosophical Psychology* 27(3): 328–50.

Luhrmann, Tanya. (2012). *When God Talks Back*, New York, Knopf.

(2020). *How God Becomes Real*, Princeton, Princeton University Press.

Machuca, Diego. (2011). "The Pyrrhonian Argument from Possible Disagreement," *Archiv für Geschichte der Philosophie* 93(2): 148–61.

Maitzen, Stephen. (2007). "Skeptical Theism and God's Commands," *Sophia* 46: 237–43.

Matheson, Jonathan. (2015). "Are Conciliatory Views of Disagreement Self-Defeating?" *Social Epistemology* 29(2): 145–59.

Mawson, T. J. (2018). *The Divine Attributes*, Cambridge, Cambridge University Press.

Meeker, Kevin. (2004). "Justification and the Social Nature of Knowledge," *Philosophy and Phenomenological Research* 69: 156–72.

McBrayer, Justin & Daniel Howard-Snyder. (2013). *The Blackwell Companion to the Problem of Evil*, West Sussex, Wiley-Blackwell.

McCauley, Robert. (2011). *Why Religion is Natural and Science is Not*, New York, Oxford University Press.

McGrew, Timothy & Linda McGrew. (2003). "The Argument from Miracles: a Cumulative Case for the Resurrection of Jesus of Nazareth," in William Lane Craig & J. P. Moreland, eds., *The Blackwell Companion to Natural Theology*, Malden, Wiley-Blackwell, pp. 593–662.

Milburn, Joe. (2023). "Unpossessed Evidence: What's the Problem?" *Topoi* 42: 107–20.

Moon, Andrew. (2021). "Circular and Question-Begging Responses to Religious Disagreement and Debunking Arguments," *Philosophical Studies* 178: 785–809.

Moser, Paul. (2010). *The Evidence for God*, Cambridge, Cambridge University Press.

(2017). "The Inner Witness of the Spirit," in William Abraham & Frederick Aquino, eds., *The Oxford Handbook of the Epistemology of Theology*, New York, Oxford University Press, pp. 111–25.

Nagasawa, Yujin. (2017). *Maximal God: A New Defense of Perfect Being Theism*, Oxford, Oxford University Press.

Newbigin, Lesslie. (1989). *The Gospel in a Pluralist Society*, Grand Rapids, Eerdmans.

Norenzayan, Ara. (2013). *Big Gods*, Princeton, Princeton University Press.

O'Connor, David. (2013). "Theistic Objections to Skeptical Theism," in Justin McBrayer & Daniel Howard-Snyder, eds., *The Blackwell Companion to the Problem of Evil*, Malden, Wiley- Blackwell, pp. 468–81.

Oppy, Graham. (2006). *Arguing About Gods*, Cambridge, Cambridge University Press.

(2014). *Describing Gods: An Investigation of Divine Attributes*, Cambridge, Cambridge University Press.

Pace, Michael. (2011). "The Epistemic Value of Moral Considerations: Justification, Moral Encroachment, and James's 'Will to Believe'," *Nous* 45(2): 239–68.

Pennock, Robert. (2001). *Intelligent Design Creationism and Its Critics*, Cambridge, MA, MIT Press.

Piazza, Tommaso. (2021). "Epistemic Defeaters," *Routledge Encyclopedia of Philosophy*. Taylor and Francis. www.rep.routledge.com/articles/thematic/epistemic-defeaters/v-1.doi:10.4324/9780415249126-P080-1

Pittard, John. (2014). "Conciliationism and Religious Disagreement," in Michael Bergmann & Patrick Kain, eds., *Challenges to Moral and Religious Belief: Disagreement and Evolution*, Oxford, Oxford University Press, 80–97.

(2020). *Disagreement, Deference, and Religious Commitment*, New York, Oxford University Press.

Plantinga, Alvin. (1981). "Is Belief in God Properly Basic?" *Nous* 15(1): 41–51.

(1993). *Warrant and Proper Function*, New York, Oxford University Press.

(2000). *Warranted Christian Belief*, New York, Oxford University Press.

(2015). *Knowledge and Christian Belief*, Grand Rapids, Eerdmans.

Pollock, John. (1987). "Defeasible Reasoning," *Cognitive Science* 11: 481–518.

Pollock, John & Cruz, Joseph. (1999). *Contemporary Theories of Knowledge*, 2nd ed., Lanham, Rowman and Littlefield.

Poston, Ted. (2014). "Skeptical Theism Within Reason," in Trent Dougherty & Justin McBrayer, eds., *Skeptical Theism: New Essays*, New York, Oxford University Press, pp. 307–22.

Price, H. H. (1965). "Belief 'In' and Belief 'That'," *Religious Studies* 1: 1–27.

Rea, Michael. (2013). "Skeptical Theism and the 'Too Much Skepticism' Objection," in Justin McBrayer & Daniel Howard-Snyder, eds., *The Blackwell Companion to the Problem of Evil*, Malden, Wiley-Blackwell, 482–506.

(2018). *The Hiddenness of God*, New York, Oxford University Press.

Schellenberg, J. L. (1993). *Divine Hiddenness and Human Reason*, Ithaca, Cornell University Press.

(2007). *The Wisdom to Doubt: A Justification of Religious Skepticism*, Ithaca, Cornell University Press.

Shermer, Michael. (2003). *How We Believe*, 2nd ed., New York, Owl Books/ Holt and Company.

Shtulman, Andrew. (2012). "Epistemic Similarities Between Students' Scientific and Supernatural Beliefs," *Journal of Educational Psychology* 105 (1): 199–212.

Slone, D. Jason. (2004). *Theological Incorrectness: Why Religious People Believe What They Shouldn't*, New York, Oxford University Press.

Smith, Christian. (2017). *Religion: What it is, How it Works, and Why it Matters*, Princeton, Princeton University Press.

Sober, Elliott. (2019). *The Design Argument*, Cambridge, Cambridge University Press.

Speaks, Jeff. (2018). *The Greatest Possible Being*, New York, Oxford University Press.

Stausberg, Michael, ed. (2009). *Contemporary Theories of Religion*, New York, Routledge.

Sudduth, Michael. (2022). "Defeaters in Epistemology," *Internet Encyclopedia of Philosophy*, ISSN 2161–0002, https://iep.utm.edu/defeaters-in-epistemology.

Swinburne, Richard. (2001). *Epistemic Justification*, Oxford, Oxford University Press.

(2003). *The Resurrection of God Incarnate*, Oxford, Oxford University Press.

(2004). *The Existence of God*, 2nd ed., Oxford, Oxford University Press.

(2005). *Faith and Reason*, 2nd ed., Oxford, Oxford University Press.

(2016). *The Coherence of Theism*, 2nd ed., Oxford, Oxford University Press.

Taylor, Charles. (2007). *A Secular Age*, Cambridge, Belknap Press/Harvard University Press.

Tersman, Folke. (2015). "Debunking and Disagreement," *Nous* 51(4): 754–74.

Thornhill-Miller, Branden & Peter Millican. (2015). "The Common-Core/Diversity Dilemma: Revisions of Humean Thought, New Empirical Research, and the Limits of Rational Religious Belief," *European Journal for Philosophy of Religion* 7(1): 1–49.

Thurow, Joshua. (2012). "Does Religious Disagreement Actually Aid the Case for Theism?" in Jake Chandler & Victoria Harrison, eds., *Probability in the Philosophy of Religion*, Oxford, Oxford University Press, 209–24.

(2013). "Does Cognitive Science Show Belief in God to be Irrational? The Epistemic Consequences of the Cognitive Science of Religion," *International Journal for Philosophy of Religion* 74: 77–98.

(2014a). "Does the Scientific Study of Religion Cast Doubt on Theistic Belief?" in Michael Bergmann & Patrick Kain, eds., *Challenges to Moral and Religious Belief: Disagreement and Evolution*, Oxford, Oxford University Press, 277–94.

(2014b). "Some Reflections on Cognitive Science, Doubt, and Religious Belief," in Roger Trigg & Justin L. Barrett, eds., *The Roots of Religion: Exploring the Cognitive Science of Religion*, Farnham, Ashgate Press, 189–207.

(2018). "Debunking and Fully Apt Belief," *Filosofia Unisinos* 19(3): 294–301.

(2023a). "Rationalization, Reasons, and Religion," in Diego Machuca, ed., *Evolutionary Debunking Arguments*, New York, Routledge, 129–59.

(2023b). "Debunking Arguments and Religious Belief," in Jonathan Fuqua, John Greco & Tyler Dalton McNabb, eds., *The Cambridge Handbook of Religious Epistemology*, Cambridge, Cambridge University Press, 290–304.

Tooley, Michael. (2019). *The Problem of Evil*, Cambridge, Cambridge University Press.

Van Inwagen, Peter. (2005). "Is God an Unnecessary Hypothesis?" in Andrew Dole & Andrew Chignell, eds., *God and the Ethics of Belief*, Cambridge, Cambridge University Press: 131–49.

(2008). *The Problem of Evil*, New York, Oxford University Press.

(2009). "Explaining Belief in the Supernatural," in Jeffrey Schloss & Michael Murray, eds., *The Believing Primate*, New York, Oxford University Press: 128–38.

Weidner, Veronika. (2021). *Divine Hiddenness*, Cambridge, Cambridge University Press.

White, Claire. (2021). *An Introduction to the Cognitive Science of Religion*, New York, Routledge.

Wiebe, Phillip. (1997). *Visions of Jesus*, New York, Oxford University Press.

Willard, Dallas. (2012). *Hearing God*, Downers Grove, Intervarsity Press.

Wilks, Ian. (2013). "The Global Skepticism Objection to Skeptical Theism," in Justin McBrayer & Daniel Howard-Snyder, eds., *The Blackwell Companion to the Problem of Evil*, Malden, Wiley-Blackwell, 458–67.

Wilkins, J. & Griffiths, P. (2012). "Evolutionary Debunking Arguments in Three Domains: Fact, Value, and Religion," in G. Dawes & J. Maclaurin, eds., *A New Science of Religion*, New York, Routledge, 133–46.

Williams, Thomas. (2014). "Describing God," in Robert Pasnau & Christian van Dyke, eds., *Cambridge History of Medieval Philosophy*, Cambridge, Cambridge University Press, 749–60.

Williamson, Timothy. (2000). *Knowledge and its Limits*, Oxford, Oxford University Press.

(2015). "Knowledge First," in Matthias Steup, John Turri, and Ernest Sosa, eds., *Contemporary Debates in Epistemology*, 2nd ed., Malden, Wiley-Blackwell: 1–9.

Wuthnow, Robert. (2012). *The God Problem: Expressing Faith and Being Reasonable*, Berkeley, University of California Press.

Acknowledgments

Thanks to Michael Almeida for discussion about some of the arguments in this Element. Thanks to Michael Peterson for patience. Thanks to Melissa Elston for stylistic suggestions and for her unwavering love. I dedicate this Element to my father, Rory Thurow, who passed away unexpectedly while I was writing it. My love for you, Dad, is and will always remain undefeated.

Cambridge Elements ≡

The Problems of God

Series Editor

Michael L. Peterson

Asbury Theological Seminary

Michael L. Peterson is Professor of Philosophy at Asbury Theological Seminary. He is the author of *God and Evil* (Routledge); *Monotheism, Suffering, and Evil* (Cambridge University Press); *With All Your Mind* (University of Notre Dame Press); *C. S. Lewis and the Christian Worldview* (Oxford University Press); *Evil and the Christian God* (Baker Book House); and *Philosophy of Education: Issues and Options* (Intervarsity Press). He is co-author of *Reason and Religious Belief* (Oxford University Press); *Science, Evolution, and Religion: A Debate about Atheism and Theism* (Oxford University Press); and *Biology, Religion, and Philosophy* (Cambridge University Press). He is editor of *The Problem of Evil: Selected Readings* (University of Notre Dame Press). He is co-editor of *Philosophy of Religion: Selected Readings* (Oxford University Press) and *Contemporary Debates in Philosophy of Religion* (Wiley-Blackwell). He served as General Editor of the Blackwell monograph series Exploring Philosophy of Religion and is founding Managing Editor of the journal *Faith and Philosophy.*

About the Series

This series explores problems related to God, such as the human quest for God or gods, contemplation of God, and critique and rejection of God. Concise, authoritative volumes in this series will reflect the methods of a variety of disciplines, including philosophy of religion, theology, religious studies, and sociology.

Cambridge Elements ≡

The Problems of God

Elements in the Series

A full series listing is available at: www.cambridge.org/EPOG